THE FLORIDA DOMICILE HANDBOOK

THE FLORIDA DOMICILE HANDBOOK:
VITAL INFORMATION FOR NEW FLORIDA RESIDENTS

2nd Edition

E. Michael Kilbourn & Brad A. Galbraith

Brendan Kelly Publishing Inc.
2122 Highview Drive
Burlington, Ontario L7R 3X4
Canada
www.brendankellypublishing.com

ISBN 978-1-895997-36-1

Printed in Canada

Mixed Sources
Product group from well-managed
forests, and other controlled sources
www.fsc.org Cert no. SW-COC-002358
© 1996 Forest Stewardship Council
FSC

To Mauri – my wife and business partner

– the one I can always count on to be there

for me and the one who inspires me to be

the best I can be.

– Mike

ACKNOWLEDGMENTS

No book worthy of reading is written without help. *The Florida Domicile Handbook: Vital Information for New Florida Residents, 2nd Edition* is no exception. Brad Galbraith and I are fortunate to have two excellent assistants, Lisa Ferguson and Joan Gardner, respectively. They deserve credit for their help in transcribing, editing, verifying and helping us with our organization of the material. Mollie Page, my friend, publicist and marketing consultant, is an extraordinary editor. Without her, the first edition could not have been written. Her additional contributions to completing the second edition are much appreciated. We are also thankful to Brendan Kelly, our publisher, for going beyond the norm to make both editions more fun and easier to read. We cannot thank Lisa, Joan, Mollie and Brendan enough for their help in making *The Florida Domicile Handbook, 2nd Edition* a book that readers will appreciate and enjoy!

The State of Florida and their myflorida.com Web site is a trove of great information that inspired and validated much of the information in this book.

I also want to thank Howard Hujsa, who inspired me to start writing *The Florida Domicile Handbook* and co-authored the first edition. His review of my work along with his corrections and additions helped make the first edition a success and paved the way for this updated edition.

CONTENTS

CONTENTS

CONTENTS

CONTENTS

CONTENTS

CONTENTS

CONTENTS

CONTENTS

PREFACE

WELCOME TO PARADISE

Picture yourself in a tropical paradise, strolling barefoot along an endless white beach. Palm trees sway in the breeze and exotic flowers bloom all around you. You enjoy countless natural wonders, recreational opportunities and warm breezes on the land and water, year-round.

Does it all sound too good to be true? It's not. Florida residents know it is not only true, but is available right outside their doors.

With an average high temperature of 80 degrees and the average low a comfortable 65, the Florida climate allows its residents to take advantage of every season. While northerners huddle indoors and dream of spring, Floridians can snorkel in the Keys in December, lay down for a tan in January and swim with dolphins in February.

Although your neighbors in the north may not realize that Florida offers many cosmopolitan opportunities, they don't know what you know. Some of the nation's top celebrities have already discovered that Florida has what it takes to support modern, stylish living. In all regions of the state, trendy cities, cultural expressions, national sports teams and outdoor recreation await new Floridians.

For its residents, Florida provides the ideal climate for living. In addition to over 1,000 miles of resplendent beaches to discover, Florida residents enjoy world-famous theme parks, sophisticated shopping destinations, unique cultural arts attractions and unparalleled golf courses located throughout the state. With a cornucopia of recreational possibilities, when it comes time to play, Floridians are never idle for lack of something fun to do.

And while Florida's climate and lifestyle benefits are plentiful and obvious, the state's residents also enjoy significant financial advantages, including:

- No state income tax
- Helpful asset protection laws
- No state estate or gift taxes
- No intangibles tax
- A favorable homestead exemption
- An annual cap on tax increases on your homestead valuation
- Portability of your savings on valuation when you relocate
- Estate planning advantages
- A friendly, pro-business environment

In the following pages, you will learn more about these and other financial incentives and how to enjoy these benefits yourself with step-by-step instructions on establishing domicile in Florida. Also included are question-and-answer formatted chapters for quick reference and answers to the most frequently asked questions on important Florida resident topics.

In addition, you will find sidebars throughout the book that have more information about the unique history, economic opportunity, relaxed lifestyle, and natural and cultural attractions that make Florida such an appealing place to call home.

With this book as your guide, you can join the growing ranks of Floridians who have realized that paradise can, indeed, be a reality.

Reprinted with permission of BigStockPhoto

INTRODUCTION

A BRIEF HISTORY OF FLORIDA

The first settlers to Florida arrived about 12,000 years ago. Florida had a much larger landmass then, nearly double the size of what it is today. The people of Florida were hunter-gatherers, depending on fruits, nuts, animals and shellfish for food. Eventually, they developed an agricultural system and began bartering with neighbors to the north in the area now known as Georgia and the Carolinas.

Between April 2 and April 8, 1513, Juan Ponce de León arrived on the east coast of Florida, in a little inlet near Daytona Beach, approximately fifty miles south of St. Augustine. He declared the new land Pascua Florida, or "Feast of Flowers," to commemorate the Easter celebration in Spain. According to popular legend, Ponce de León discovered Florida while on his expedition to find the Fountain of Youth. Ponce de León returned to Florida in 1521 with other settlers to start a colony, but failed because of attacks from Native Americans.

In 1539, Hernando de Soto, also a Spaniard, made another attempt at colonization. De Soto came to Florida in search of gold and silver. His expedition did not last long though. After three years of searching the southwestern coastline, de Soto died near the Mississippi River area in 1542.

Not long after de Soto's death, more attempts at colonization by the Spaniards and French followed. In 1562, Frenchman Jean Ribault explored the northeastern area of Florida. In 1564, René Goulaine de Laudonnière, an associate of Ribault, colonized Fort Caroline, which is now known as Jacksonville. Soon, many Catholic churches were built in Florida. French colonization inspired the Spaniards to populate the area aggressively. Pedro Menéndez de Avilès landed in Florida in 1565 and claimed St. Augustine, which is the oldest permanent European settlement in the United States. Menéndez de Avilès took over Fort Caroline, killing the French soldiers and renaming it San Mateo. After two years, the French came back to San Mateo, recaptured it and killed all the Spaniards.

In 1763, Spain traded Florida to the British for Havana, Cuba. After the trade, all Spaniards evacuated Florida. Britain divided Florida into East and West Florida, with capitals in St. Augustine and Pensacola. In an attempt to attract more British settlers to Florida, the British decided to offer land for free to those who would export products. During the American Revolutionary War in 1784, Spain allied with France and temporarily regained control of Florida.

In an effort to repopulate the area, Spain offered land grants to people of the United States. In 1818, the Seminole tribe tried to regain the land from these settlers, starting the First Seminole War.

Spain eventually relinquished Florida and in 1821 it became a U.S. territory. Tallahassee became the new capital because it was halfway between the two former capitals. General Andrew Jackson served as military governor until Congress ratified a territorial constitution. William P. Duval, Florida's first civil governor, called the first Legislative Council into session in Pensacola on June 19, 1823. Its popularity grew and Florida started to attract southern plantation owners. As they continued to move into Florida, the demand for land started to increase. The Seminole leader, Osceola, refused to give up his tribe's land and started the Second Seminole War. In the end, the Indians were forced out. While some left voluntarily, others escaped south to the Everglades.

In 1845, Florida became the twenty-seventh state to join the United States of America. During the presidential election of 1860, there were no Florida votes for Abraham Lincoln. Shortly after his election, Florida became a part of the Confederate States of America. During the Civil War, residents supplied Confederate troops with food, men and cotton. Located just outside Lake City, the Olustee Battlefield State Historic Site commemorates the largest battle fought in Florida during the American Civil War. Interestingly, Tallahassee was the only capital of a Confederate state east of the Mississippi not captured by Union forces. Even though the Confederacy was defeated in 1865, Florida's economy continued to grow as it exported lumber and other materials and developed a large-scale cattle industry.

In the late 1800s, Florida development was on the rise. Railroads expanded into the area and many people came to live and visit such cities as Tampa, West Palm Beach and Winter Park. In the 1920s, land sales skyrocketed. The Great Depression and several hurricanes hurt Florida's economy and slowed settlement, but the popularity of Florida began to flourish again with the creation of major theme parks in the 1930s. The first theme park, Cypress Gardens, was built in Central Florida.

By the 1950s, Florida's land boom was back on, spurred by World War II and road construction. In the 1960s, Walt Disney brought his dream to Florida and began building Walt Disney World in Central Florida. At present, the theme park industry continues to develop and tourism is one of the most significant financial industries in Florida.

A Map of Florida in 1870

Migration continues to expand in impressive numbers throughout all areas of Florida. Low taxes and a warm climate are the primary reasons why people move to this subtropical paradise. It is no surprise that many major U.S. corporations have also chased the migration southward and chosen to move their headquarters to Florida.

" WE LIKE TO SPEND 51 WEEKS OF THE
YEAR AT OUR FLORIDA
HOLIDAY HOME... "

PART 1

BENEFITS OF FLORIDA DOMICILE

D id you know that approximately 70 percent of Florida's population was born elsewhere? Interestingly, studies show that most newcomers emigrate from the eastern and mid-western states of New York, New Jersey, Pennsylvania, the District of Columbia, Maryland, Illinois, Indiana, Michigan, Ohio and Wisconsin. While most newcomers become permanent year-round residents, others simply enjoy a part-time or seasonal residency.

Upon arrival and exploration of the tropical landscape, visitors quickly realize the top three reasons for moving to Florida are weather, low taxes and recreation. However, as discussed throughout this book, there are many other great incentives for making Florida your permanent home. It is common knowledge that Florida has very attractive winters, but many are also discovering that the living costs are significantly less than in other warm destinations – in part, explaining why more than three times as many retirees choose Florida over California.

The question isn't at what age I want to retire,
it's at what income.
– George Foreman

CHAPTER 1

THE FLORIDA ADVANTAGE

Tax Advantages

Florida is one of the few states that does not impose an income tax on its residents. In 2007, Florida eliminated its intangible personal property tax, making it one of the most tax-friendly states in the country. In fact, Florida ranks thirteenth of the fifty states for its low tax burden, with only Texas, Alabama and New Mexico having lower tax burden percentages of any southern state.

A provision in the Economic Growth and Tax Relief Reconciliation Act of 2001 eliminated the sharing of federal estate tax revenues with the states. Consequently, many states adopted a separate form of estate tax, whereas Florida did not. And, no matter what happens on the federal level, Florida is constitutionally bound to allow its citizens to decide their fate regarding a state estate tax through the constitutional amendment process. As a result, it seems extremely unlikely that Florida will ever have a separate estate tax. You will discover more Florida tax benefits in Chapter 2.

Asset Protection Advantages

When you are domiciled in Florida, certain assets are protected from the claims of your creditors. Such assets include your homestead, retirement plans, life insurance, annuities, assets held in a properly structured Florida corporation, limited liability company, certain types of partnerships and, in many cases, wage accounts. This protection is generally unlimited; however, many advantages of asset protection are not available or are limited when personal bankruptcy is involved.

For instance, retirement plans, including individual retirement accounts (IRAs) and Roth IRA accounts, are normally protected from attachment by creditors in Florida. In the case of IRAs and Roth IRA accounts, if a bankruptcy is involved, the amount exempted under the 2005 Bankruptcy law is limited to one million dollars unless the owner can demonstrate that the excess amount represents rollover distributions from one or more qualified retirement plans.

An in depth explanation of the major financial benefits of Florida domicile, such as asset protection strategies surrounding annuities, assets held in a properly structured Florida corporation, limited liability company and certain types of partnerships and, in many cases, wage accounts, is contained in Chapter 4.

The Real Estate Market

Real estate values indicate that Florida is one of the most desirable locations in the world. According to the Florida Association of Realtors, there are over 90,000 registered Realtors in the state vying to sell thousands of homes where the median price in 2010 was around $138,000.

Donald Trump bought his seven-acre oceanfront estate in Palm Beach for $41 million in 2004 and later listed it for sale for $125 million. Even if your budget isn't of this magnitude, finding your dream home in paradise is not impossible. Since 2006, the real estate market has declined and mortgage interest rates have reached new lows. The real estate market has shifted from being a seller's market to being a buyer's market. With the buying tips we provide in Chapter 10, you will discover how to search, negotiate and borrow so that you too can own a piece of paradise.

Property Tax Advantages

Another Florida tax advantage is provided in the mechanism for assessing real estate property taxes. Residents can limit their exposure to increased real estate taxes on their homes through the homestead exemption and the special component known as the Save Our Homes Amendment to the Florida Constitution which is covered in Chapter 3.

After you purchase a home and declare your Florida domicile, you may qualify for a homestead tax exemption of $25,000 by simply applying for the exemption. As of January 1, 2008, you may also qualify for an additional $25,000 homestead exemption for non-school taxes on homesteads with assessed values above $75,000. Depending upon the Florida county where you establish your domicile, the standard exemption for those who qualify, typically saves approximately $300 to $500 in property taxes per year. The combination of the two exemptions will generally save approximately $400 to $800 in property taxes per year. Low-income seniors and certain disabled veterans can receive additional Florida homestead benefits. More information about the advantages of Florida's homestead exemption laws, including the "Save Our Homes" amendment, is contained in Chapter 3.

Estate Planning Advantages

Floridians are fortunate to have a significant number of top financial advisers and estate planning professionals who can assist in managing and planning your estate. Yet, in order to properly protect yourself and your family, you must have an understanding of estate planning and the options available to you. Issues to understand and consider include probate avoidance, federal estate tax minimization, planning for disability from both a financial and health care perspective, eventual distribution options and protection available to beneficiaries, and what must be done to keep your plan up-to-date. These topics and many others are discussed in Chapter 4.

INTERESTING FLORIDA FACTS

Nickname: "The Sunshine State"

State motto: "In God We Trust"

State flower: Orange Blossom (Citrus sinensis)

State bird: Mockingbird

State animal: Florida Panther

State freshwater fish: Largemouth Bass

State saltwater fish: Sailfish

State insect: Zebra Longwing Butterfly

State tree: Sabal Palm

State reptile: American Alligator

State marine mammal: West Indian Manatee

State saltwater mammal: Dolphin

State shell: Horse Conch

State anthem: "Florida (Where the Sawgrass Meets the Sky)"
  by Jan Hinton

State song: "Old Folks at Home" by Stephen Foster

State fruit: Orange

State beverage: Orange Juice

State pie: Key Lime Pie

Number of people who move to Florida each day: 1,000 (2009)

Number of major commercial airports: 19

Number of international airports: 12

Number of deepwater ports: 14

Miles of sand beaches: 663

Miles of coastline: 1,800

Number of golf courses: 1,250 and growing!

County with the most golf courses: Palm Beach County

Number of hotel rooms in Florida: 370,000+

Number of campgrounds: 700 (100,000 campsites)

Number of people camping in Florida each year: 6 million

Source: Florida Dept. of State; Visit Florida; www.myflorida.com; U.S. Census Bureau; Bureau of Economic & Business Research (University of Florida); State of Florida.com research, National Golf Foundation.

Career Opportunities

With so many people choosing to make Florida their home and so many businesses relocating to the Sunshine State, there are constantly increasing options for those seeking employment and career opportunities. Appendix A lists several Web sites, e.g. www.jobs.careerbuilder.com, that specialize in helping you find job opportunities.

Even More Advantages

There are as many advantages to moving to Florida now and declaring it your domicile as there are in spending your fun-filled days under the Florida sun.

In order to provide you with comprehensive information that will make changing your domicile to Florida easier, we have included chapters on Florida Driver Licenses and Motor Vehicles (Chapter 7), Florida Insurance and Health Care Options (Chapter 11), Registering to Vote in Florida (Chapter 8), and Florida Education Options (Chapter 12). In the following pages, we hope you will discover a wealth of Florida facts and trivia that will inspire you to live your Florida life to its fullest.

10 COMMON FLORIDA MYTHS

MYTH 1: Sharks attack Florida beachgoers.
FACT: The possibility of a shark attack in Florida is almost nonexistent. Millions of beachgoers safely enjoy Florida's beaches every year. In fact, according to the Florida Museum of Natural History, between 1959 and 2007 there were 449 fatalities from lightning versus 8 from shark attacks in Florida.

MYTH 2: Florida has very little to offer in the way of new jobs.
FACT: Florida has all the makings of a job-creating machine: excellent weather, low costs, growing population, strong tourism industry and little heavy manufacturing. Based on a report by the State of Florida Agency for Workforce, the following occupations lead the list of jobs in demand in Florida as of 2010: Computer Software Engineers, Dental Hygienists, Medical Assistants, Data Communications Analysts and Physical Therapist Assistants.

MYTH 3: Florida is nothing but boring retirement homes.
FACT: Florida supports a variety of upscale lifestyles from stylish communities complete with world-class golf courses to fine dining and national sports franchises (Florida is the only state with three NFL teams). So it is easy to lead an active life in Florida. What to do? Choose from over 1,200 golf courses, over 8,000 large fishing lakes, numerous upscale shopping destinations and much more.

MYTH 4: There's nothing cultural in Florida.
FACT: Florida offers much more than just jai alai for the cosmopolitan resident. It is home to a colorful array of local artists and writers like novelists Carl Hiaasen, Randy Wayne White, Dave Barry, Tim Dorsey and James W. Hall. Creativity and the arts permeate the state. There are symphonies in all the major cities, art galleries, festivals and theater options from major touring productions to cutting-edge playhouses. It's no surprise that Sarasota is frequently ranked as one of the top arts communities in the nation.

10 COMMON FLORIDA MYTHS

MYTH 5: My Florida home will be blown away by a hurricane.
FACT: Despite impressive news footage, most homes never have to weather a hurricane's direct hit. Since Hurricane Andrew in 1992, building codes have improved and, if they have to, new homes can weather all but the most extreme storms. But that probably won't happen. According to the National Oceanic and Atmospheric Administration (NOAA) statistics, fewer than half of the hurricanes that have struck Florida in the last century were classified as major storms.

MYTH 6: Florida is full of swamps, alligators and snakes.
FACT: Florida has swamps, alligators and snakes, but they don't live where you do. When looking for wild recreation, you can visit the Everglades and other natural parks, but residential areas are on higher ground where swamp critters rarely venture. If an alligator takes up residence in a water hazard, suburban lake or other unsuitable location, county officials and experienced animal trappers are available to quickly remove it.

MYTH 7: You will contract a debilitating disease like encephalitis if a mosquito in Florida bites you.
FACT: Part of local governments' duties in Florida is to control mosquitoes. In Southwest Florida, the Mosquito Control District uses the latest in science and technology to spray for adult mosquitoes and kill larva before they hatch. Such active control keeps urban areas relatively free from bugs. And because only certain species of mosquito can transmit certain diseases, mosquito control districts aggressively target them. Combined with careful monitoring of sentry animals, mosquito control prevents the outbreak of mosquito-borne sickness.

10 COMMON FLORIDA MYTHS

MYTH 8: If you live in Florida, you'll get skin cancer.
FACT: It is true that Florida has lots of sun, but you always have a choice when it comes to turning into a human baked potato. There's a reason sunscreen was invented in Miami in 1944. Simply lather up, wear a hat and enjoy the year-round sunshine.

MYTH 9: No one speaks English in Florida.
FACT: Like many other states, Florida is a diverse melting pot, no question. And although the Hispanic population is growing fast, according to census data, the majority of foreign-born residents who speak a different language at home speak English "well" or "very well." You won't have trouble finding businesses that speak your language.

MYTH 10: Aside from tourism, Florida is an orange grove.
FACT: Citrus and tourism are big business in Florida, but there is much more to it than that. According to the Florida Cybercities 2007 report, Florida is ranked as the fourth state in total employment in high-tech industries. In fact, Orlando is home to a thriving film industry and, thanks to the Mayo Clinic, the Cleveland Clinic and several world-class universities, it is also respected for its major medical advances. With a pro-business climate, Florida's economy is exciting and varied, from national companies to small mom-and-pop businesses.

FLORIDA: A GOLFER'S DREAM

With more golf courses than any other destination in the world, it is no wonder golfers choose Florida as the place to vacation and, ultimately, reside. From Pensacola to Key West and from Jacksonville to Naples, Florida has more than 1,250 courses to test the skill level of any player. And Florida's climate allows you to enjoy the sport 365 days a year.

If you just like to watch, Florida is home to the PGA Tour, Champions Tour, LPGA, PGA of America, World Golf Hall of Fame and several other professional golf tours. In fact, more professional golfers live in Florida than in any other state.

Founded in 1916, The PGA of America is the largest working sports organization in the world, comprised of more than 28,000 dedicated men and women promoting the game of golf to everyone, everywhere. Discover tournaments in Florida at www.pga.com.

The Club at Pelican Bay in Naples

photo courtesy of Teresa Kelly

I am proud to be paying taxes in the United States. The only
thing is I could be just as proud for half of the money.
— Arthur Godfrey

CHAPTER 2

FLORIDA TAXES

E ven with a state budget in 2010 of $66.5 billion, one of the most attractive financial reasons to choose Florida as your domicile is the relatively low taxes. Depending on the state you are moving from, the tax relief may be significant.

Florida provides an ideal tax climate for both retirees and businesses. The state ranks low in terms of the tax burden placed on residents. Based on income, property and other state and local tax collections, the Tax Foundation—a nonpartisan educational organization that helps consumers understand tax policy—ranked Florida among the states with the lowest state tax burden. Estimated at 7.4 percent of income, Florida's state/local tax burden percentage is ranked forty-seventh nationally, well below the national average of 9.7 percent. The elimination of Florida's intangibles tax in 2007 will likely improve Florida's ranking even further, compared to the total tax burden of other states.

No Income Tax

Florida is one of only nine states, including Alaska, Nevada, New Hampshire, South Dakota, Tennessee, Texas, Washington and Wyoming, without a personal income tax. This benefit alone could be reason enough to make Florida your permanent domicile and may represent substantial savings to you and your family. No income tax means the revenue you generate from employment and your investment earnings is free to grow without the burden of a high state-imposed tax rate. For example, if your domicile is Vermont, the tax ranges from 3.6 to 9.5 percent depending on the level of your income each year.

Interestingly, imposing a state income tax is specifically prohibited by the Florida Constitution and it's unlikely that the voters of Florida will ever vote to add a state income tax.

To look at an example, let's assume that in 2010 a married couple had $70,000 each in wages plus $10,000 in combined interest income for a total adjusted gross income (AGI) of $150,000. Suppose also that they had no itemized deductions. The state income tax for Florida is zero. However, in many other states the picture, as shown below, is quite different:

Michigan tax = $6,525 (flat tax at 4.35% of $150,000)
California tax = $11,323 (graduated tax)
Pennsylvania tax = $4,605 (flat tax at 3.07% of $150,000)

If that same couple, domiciled in Florida, received a salary or rental income from real estate located in a different state, the other state may impose its own income tax (though Florida would not).

No Inheritance or Gift Tax

The federal government no longer shares estate tax revenues with the states (see next page). In response, many states have "decoupled" from the federal estate tax system, meaning that those states have established their own gift and estate (and/or inheritance) taxes.

Florida is one of only three states whose state constitution requires voter approval for the imposition of a state inheritance or gift tax. Consequently, Florida has no current estate or gift taxes and is unlikely to have any in the future—without a change in the Florida Constitution by Florida voters. This could provide substantial savings for your heirs.

CHAPTER 2: FLORIDA TAXES

STATE	INHERITANCE TAX?	ESTATE TAX?
Alabama	No	No
Alaska	No	No
Arizona	No	No
Arkansas	No	No
California	No	No
Colorado	No	No
Connecticut	**Yes**	No
Delaware	No	No
District of Columbia	No	**Yes**
FLORIDA	NO	NO
Georgia	No	No
Hawaii	No	No
Idaho	No	No
Illinois	No	**Yes**
Indiana	**Yes**	No
Iowa	**Yes**	No
Kansas	**Yes**	**Yes**
Kentucky	**Yes**	No
Louisiana	No	No
Maine	No	**Yes**
Maryland	**Yes**	**Yes**
Massachusetts	No	**Yes**
Michigan	No	No
Minnesota	No	**Yes**
Mississippi	No	No
Missouri	No	No
Montana	No	No
Nebraska	**Yes**	**Yes**
Nevada	No	No
New Hampshire	No	No
New Jersey	**Yes**	**Yes**
New Mexico	No	No
New York	No	**Yes**
North Carolina	No	**Yes**
North Dakota	No	No
Ohio	No	**Yes**
Oklahoma	No	No
Oregon	**Yes**	**Yes**
Pennsylvania	**Yes**	No
Rhode Island	No	**Yes**
South Carolina	No	No
South Dakota	No	No
Tennessee	**Yes**	No
Texas	No	No
Utah	No	No
Vermont	No	**Yes**
Virginia	No	**Yes**
Washington	No	**Yes**
West Virginia	No	No
Wisconsin	No	**Yes**
Wyoming	No	No

For example, Maryland has decoupled from the federal estate tax system and now levies a separate state inheritance tax. So, if you are domiciled in Maryland, your heirs may face an inheritance tax of 16 percent on assets above Maryland's applicable exclusion amount, which is only $1,000,000. The tax computed would be in addition to any federal estate tax due.

Note that even though Florida does not impose its own estate or gift tax, if you own real estate or tangible assets in another state, your heirs may be subject to an estate tax in the other state.

As seen in the chart on the previous page, eleven states collect an inheritance tax. They are: Connecticut, Indiana, Iowa, Kansas, Kentucky, Maryland, Nebraska, New Jersey, Oregon, Pennsylvania and Tennessee.

Seventeen states and the District of Columbia have retained their estate taxes after the federal changes. Of these, 15 states – Illinois, Kansas, Maine, Maryland, Massachusetts, Minnesota, New Jersey, New York, North Carolina, Ohio, Oregon, Rhode Island, Vermont, Virginia, and Wisconsin – and the District of Columbia decoupled from the federal changes. Two states (Nebraska and Washington) retained their tax by enacting similar but separate estate taxes.

No Intangibles Tax

An intangibles tax is a state tax on intangible assets, such as stocks, bonds, notes, etc. In 2006, the Florida legislature and the governor repealed the state's long-standing Florida intangibles tax, effective January 1, 2007. Therefore, newcomers need not be concerned about filing a Florida intangibles tax form or paying any tax on intangible assets. This makes Florida one of the very few states that does not charge either an income tax or intangibles tax and, thus, Florida can truly be called a tax haven.

Sales Tax

Florida law provides that each sale, admission charge, storage fee or rental is taxable, along with some services, unless the transaction is specifically exempt. The current state sales tax rate is 6 percent. This amounts to considerably less than the average state sales tax in the United States of 7.25 percent excluding five states, like Alaska and Delaware, that have no sales tax.

Discretionary Sales Surtax

Under specific conditions, Florida counties are authorized to levy a discretionary sales surtax on most transactions that are subject to sales and use tax. The tax is determined by the county where the merchandise or service is delivered, ranges from 0.25 to 1.5 percent, and is in addition to the six percent state sales tax.

Only the first $5,000 of a single sale of tangible personal property is subject to the discretionary sales surtax if the property is sold as a single item, in bulk, as a working unit or as part of a working unit. Items that are not normally sold as a set or unit cannot be combined to qualify for the $5,000 limit and are taxed at the normal discretionary sales surtax rate. Also, the $5,000 limit does not apply to commercial rentals, transient rentals or services.

For example, a $6,000 piano delivered to a home in a Florida county imposing a 1.0 percent discretionary sales surtax would have the following tax:

$6,000 × 6% (sales tax)	$360
$5,000 × 1% (surtax)	+$50
Total tax due	**$410**

If you reside in a Florida county that imposes a surtax (which can vary from time to time) and purchase an automobile, boat or aircraft to be titled in your name, the dealer is required to collect the surtax at the county rate. For example, if you lived in one of forty-three counties, such as Miami-Dade County, in 2010 and purchased a $35,000 automobile to be titled in your name, the following tax would apply:

$35,000 × 6% (sales tax) $2,100
$5,000 × 1% (surtax)   +$ 50
Total tax due   **$2,150**

A list of Florida counties, their discretionary sales surtax rates, and appropriate dates are published each year on Form DR-15DSS. Information and forms are available online at www.myflorida.com/dor. Contact information for the Florida Department of Revenue is included at the end of this chapter.

Use Tax

Use tax complements and is applied in the same manner as sales tax. Unless specifically exempt, use tax is due on purchases made out

DISCRETIONARY SALES SURTAX ON TAXABLE ITEMS (LOCAL OPTION COUNTY TAX)

If a vendor located in any Florida county	with a discretionary surtax	sells & delivers	into the county where the selling vendor is located,	surtax is collected at the county rate where the delivery is made.
If a vendor located in any Florida county	with or without a discretionary surtax	sells & delivers	into counties with different discretionary surtax rates,	surtax is collected at the county where the delivery is made.
If a vendor located in any Florida county	with or without a discretionary surtax	sells & delivers	into counties without a discretionary surtax,	surtax is not collected.
If an out-of-state vendor		sells & delivers	into a Florida county with a discretionary surtax,	surtax is collected at the county rate where the delivery is made.
If an out-of-state vendor		sells & delivers	into a Florida county without a discretionary surtax,	surtax is not collected.

Source: Florida Department of Revenue, dor.myflorida.com/dor/taxes/discretionary.html.

of state and brought into Florida within six months of the purchase date. The use tax rate and the sales tax rate are the same, including the additional discretionary sales surtax, if applicable.

Examples of taxable purchases include such things as an automobile purchased in another state, furniture delivered from a dealer located in another state, computer equipment purchased from an out-of-state computer firm and so forth.

Purchased items used in another state for six months or longer are not subject to the use tax when they are brought into Florida. Also, no tax is due if the out-of-state dealer charged sales tax of six percent or more. If the dealer charged less than six percent, you are required to pay the difference.

For example, if, as a Florida resident, you purchased an automobile and brought it into Florida within six months after the purchase and the dealer charged four percent sales tax, you must pay the additional two percent tax to Florida. This is similar to how most other states treat the purchase of tangible personal property from other states.

To file and pay the use tax, you must complete an out-of-state purchase return form (DR-15MO). The form can be retrieved at the Web site http://dor.myflorida.com/dor/forms/2010/dr15n. pdf. For additional assistance, contact the Florida Department of Revenue at the phone numbers listed in the table at the end of this chapter.

Rent Tax

Florida home owners who rent their home, condominium or other real estate in Florida to another person for a period of six months or greater must pay a six percent tax on the amount of rent received. The additional cost is frequently passed on to the tenant as an addition to the rent paid.

For example, if you collect monthly rent of $4,000 for a home or office that you are leasing for six months or longer, the rent is taxed at the rate of six percent as follows:

Monthly tax = 6% × $4,000 = $240

Real Property (Ad Valorem) Tax

If you own a home or other real estate in Florida, the value will be assessed by the county appraiser, as of January 1 each year, and taxed by the county tax collector in the county where the property is located.

Each county determines its own millage or tax rate (per $1,000 of valuation) according to that county's budget needs. The assessed value is multiplied by the tax rate to calculate the tax which is billed in November and due by April 1 of the following year. If you build your homestead, the property appraiser will not assess its improved value until after the county issues a certificate of occupancy.

For example, if the Florida county where you own your homestead assesses the value at $500,000, less the Florida Homestead Exemption of $50,000 and the total millage rate for the current tax year is 11.5, the total current tax due would be calculated in two steps, as follows:

Homestead valuation reduction:
$500,000 - $50,000 = $450,000
Tax = 11.5 × ($450,000/$1,000) = $5,175

In order to properly calculate the school tax portion of the property tax bill, the Homestead Exemption is only $25,000.

Non-Homestead Properties

As a result of the Florida Constitutional Save Our Homes (SOH) amendment passed by voters on January 29, 2008, there is an assessment growth limitation of ten percent for all *non-homestead* properties, subject to the following limitations:

- The assessment limitation does not apply to school tax levies;
- The assessment limitation will expire in ten years from enactment at which time, voters will decide whether to reauthorize it;
- Residential properties of nine units or less will surrender accumulated protections at change of ownership or control;
- For all other properties (i.e., residential properties of ten or more units and business properties), the Legislature must define how the property will surrender protections when there is a "qualifying improvement" to the property. The Legislature *may* define how the property will surrender accumulated protections at a change of ownership or control;
- The cap uses 2008 as its base year.

Tangible Personal Property

The same Florida Constitutional SOH Amendment passed on January 29, 2008, created an exemption of $25,000 for tangible personal property for businesses. Thus, business owners with tangible personal property (i.e., computers, copiers, fax machines, etc.) worth less than $25,000 and used in their businesses do not have to file detailed returns and will owe no tax. This exemption applies to school tax levies as well.

Documentary Stamp Tax

Florida assesses a tax on promissory notes, mortgages, security agreements and other written promises to pay money. The basic tax is 35 cents per $100. On all documents that convey an interest in real estate, however, the tax is 70 cents per $100.

For example, on a $40,000 promissory note, the tax would be assessed at the rate of 35 cents per $100 of value and is calculated as follows:

Tax = $0.35 × ($40,000/$100) = $140

For large loan amounts, the documentary stamp tax is capped at $2,450.

On the transfer of a parcel of Florida real estate valued at one million dollars, the tax is based on 70 cents per $100 of value and is calculated as follows:

Tax = $0.70 × ($1,000,000/$100) = $7,000

Florida Business Taxes

While a discussion of the over thirty possible taxes affecting a Florida business is beyond the scope of this book, there are five taxes (sales and use tax, discretionary sales surtax, unemployment tax, communications services tax and corporate income tax) that are worth emphasizing, since many businesses are subject to them.

Many local agencies such as the Small Business Administration can help new residents set up a business. In addition, Department of Revenue (DOR) service centers around the state host educational

---

HILLS...IN FLORIDA

The highest point in Florida is Britton Hill in Lakewood, at 345 feet above sea level. Not only is it the highest point in Florida, but it is also the "lowest high point" in the United States. Contrary to popular belief, however, Florida is not entirely flat. Some places have hills that rise 50 to 100 feet above sea level. Much of the interior of Florida features rolling hills with elevations ranging from 100 to 250 feet.

Source: www.Gameandfishguides.com.

seminars about Florida's taxes. This could be especially helpful if you are starting a new business or planning to move your business to Florida. For a complete list of taxes administered by the Florida DOR, contact the DOR Taxpayer Services (see contact information listed at the end of this chapter).

Sales and Use Tax

Sales tax applies to the sale, rental, lease or license to use goods, certain services and commercial property in Florida, unless the transaction is specifically exempt. If your business involves taxable transactions, you must register as a sales and use tax dealer before you begin conducting business in Florida. Currently, the sales tax in Florida is set at six percent.

Dealers are responsible for collecting sales tax at the time of each sale and for remitting the tax for each collection period to the Department of Revenue, along with a Sales and Use Tax Return (Form DR-15). Any use tax due must also be accrued and remitted on your tax return. You must file even if no tax is due. If the opening date of your business changes, you must notify the DOR to avoid a notice of delinquency and a late-filing penalty.

Discretionary Sales Surtax for Businesses

As discussed previously for individuals, Florida counties are authorized to levy a discretionary sales surtax on most business transactions that occur in a county that has adopted the discretionary surtax.

A dealer who sells and delivers taxable merchandise or a taxable service to a location within a county imposing a discretionary surtax is required to collect the surtax at the rate imposed in the county where the merchandise or service is delivered. The surtax is levied on the first $5,000 of any item of tangible personal property. The $5,000 limit does not apply to commercial rentals, transient rentals or services.

Dealers remit discretionary sales surtax to the Florida Department of Revenue, along with sales and use tax, on the Sales and Use Tax Return (Form DR-15CS).

Unemployment Tax

Unemployment compensation provides partial, temporary income to workers who lose their jobs through no fault of their own and are able and available for work. The employer pays for unemployment compensation through a tax administered by the Department of Revenue.

Workers do not pay any part of the unemployment tax and employers must not make payroll deductions for this purpose. The employer's payments go into a reserve fund from which benefits are paid to eligible claimants. After a qualifying period, employers with a stable employment history will receive credit for this in a reduced tax rate.

BUSINESSES LIKE TAX-FRIENDLY FLORIDA

Florida provides an ideal climate for business. Every year, the Tax Foundation, Washington, D.C., ranks the business climate in each of the fifty states. The report compares the states in five areas of taxation that impact business: corporate taxes; individual income taxes; sales taxes; unemployment insurance taxes; and taxes on property, including residential and commercial property. In 2010, Florida had the fifth best state business tax climate, behind only Nevada, Alaska, South Dakota, and Wyoming.

In July 2010, Florida was ranked number one in the nation for its workforce by CNBC through its annual America's Top States for Business rankings. The study measured all 50 states and examined 10 different categories, including workforce, to measure each state's ability to attract businesses.

Employers are required to file an Employer's Quarterly Report (Form UCT-6) each quarter, regardless of employment activity or whether any taxes are due.

Communications Services Tax

If your business provides communications services, you must register to collect and remit communications services tax. The tax is imposed on voice, data, audio, video or any other information or signal, including cable services that are transmitted by any medium. Dealers of communications services are required to file a monthly Communications Services Tax Return (Form DR-700016).

Corporate Income Tax

S Corporations, partnerships, limited liability companies taxed as partnerships and tax-exempt organizations are generally not required to file a Florida corporate income tax return. However, if any such entity pays any federal income tax itself, it may be required to file a Florida corporate income tax return and pay any tax due.

C-Corporations that conduct business or earn or receive income in Florida must file a Florida corporate income tax return unless specifically exempted by law. The return must be filed even if no tax is due. The corporate income tax rate is 5.5% of net income. A 3.3% alternative minimum tax may also apply.

Additional Resources

More detailed information is located in the DOR Tax Rules. Call Taxpayer Services (telephone numbers on the following page) to request copies of Chapters 199, 202, 212, 220 and 443, Florida Statutes, and Rule 12A-15.002, Florida Administrative Code. Tax rules are also available on the department's Web site. Look for the Florida Tax Law Library. Additional business registration and tax forms are available at www.myflorida.com/dor/taxes/business_opp.html.

CONTACT THE DEPARTMENT OF REVENUE

General questions: 800-352-3671
Hearing/speech impaired: TDD 800-367-8331 or 850-922-1115
DOR Distribution Center: 850-488-8422

Address for a written
reply to tax questions:
Taxpayer Services
Florida Department of Revenue
5050 West Tennessee Street
Tallahassee, FL 32304-2716

Order copies online: www.myflorida.com/dor/forms
Fax form requests to: 850-922-2208

Mail form requests to:
Distribution Center
Florida Department of Revenue
168A Blountstown Hwy.
Tallahassee, FL 32304-2702

Note: Taxpayer Services is open Monday through Friday, 8 a.m. to 7 p.m., ET.

AN ENDANGERED PREDATOR

The unique and beautiful Florida panther (Puma concolor coryi) has been on the Endangered Species List since 1967. This big, graceful tan-colored cat makes its home in South Florida, where it hunts deer and other game. Much of the state's research funding to study and protect the Florida panther is financed by sales of the Florida panther specialty license plate. The main threat facing the panther today is loss of habitat. Only approximately 100 panthers remain in Florida.

Reprinted with permission of BigStockPhoto

NOTES

*A house is not a home unless it contains food
and fire for the mind as well as the body.*
— Benjamin Franklin

CHAPTER 3

FLORIDA HOMESTEAD EXEMPTION

A Florida homestead has been called a "legal chameleon" because the notion of "homestead status" may change, depending upon the situation. Florida homestead laws have three aspects that are important to residents: (1) the real estate tax exemption for homestead (commonly referred to as the homestead tax exemption) and its related component, known as the "Save Our Homes" amendment to the Florida Constitution, (2) protection from a forced sale of the homestead by a creditor (asset protection) and (3) "devise and descent" issues for a surviving spouse and minor children. All these aspects have the same purpose: to protect the owner of the homestead and his or her heirs.

Homestead Tax Exemption

A special homestead tax exemption, equal to $25,000 (the "standard" exemption), is available to any homeowner who becomes a permanent Florida resident. The exemption means the first $25,000 of value of your Florida homestead (principal residence) is not taxed. Effective since January 1, 2007, Florida voters approved two amendments that increased the standard homestead exemption amount to $50,000 for low-income seniors and provides additional homestead deductions to certain disabled veterans over 65. Effective since January 1, 2008, Florida voters approved an additional $25,000 homestead exemption for non-school taxes on homesteads that applies to homes with assessed values of $50,000 or greater.

The courts in Florida have been very generous in allowing this homestead tax exemption to apply to all sorts of home ownership, not merely for the traditional single-family home but also for condominiums, cooperative apartments and certain types of mobile homes.

For Florida residents who qualify for and have received the homestead exemption, there is a significant additional tax benefit that results from the Save Our Homes amendment to the Florida Constitution.

Save Our Homes Amendment

The Save Our Homes (SOH) amendment to the Florida Constitution is a special component of the Florida homestead exemption and could represent substantial savings over a period of years to you and your family. This amendment, which became effective January 1, 1995, places a limitation or cap on the percentage increase in annual tax assessment of the value of a residence that qualifies for the homestead exemption. The cap is the lower of the increase in the consumer price index or 3 percent of the assessed value of the home each year following the year you receive your homestead exemption.

There has been quite a bit of confusion concerning the workings of the Save Our Homes amendment. A simple example will help. Assuming you became a Florida resident on or before December 31, 2010, you would have until March 1, 2011, to file for Florida's Homestead Exemption and that exemption would be effective January 1, 2011. Although the county property appraiser may have reassessed your homestead on January 1, 2011, and increased its value to its then fair market value, the 3 percent valuation cap would apply on January 1, 2012. If, however, you had postponed becoming a Florida resident until January 2, 2011, and subsequently filed for homestead, you would not be able to secure the Homestead Exemption for that year, even if you filed for homestead by March 1, 2011 (early filing). In this case, you have until March 1, 2012, to obtain the Homestead Exemption for 2012. The 3 percent cap would come into play the following year which, in this case, would be 2013.

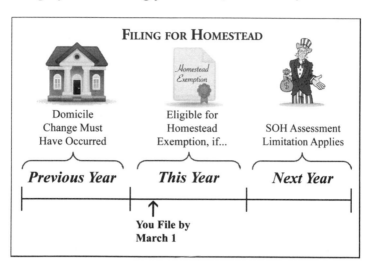

Portability

On January 29, 2008, Florida voters approved a change to the Florida Constitution that allows for the portability of accumulated SOH benefits for homeowners who move from one Florida homestead to another. The new law provides the following:

Homeowners may transfer their SOH benefit to a new homestead anywhere in Florida within two years of leaving their former homestead. For example, those who sold their homes in 2010 can transfer their SOH benefit to a new homestead if they establish the new homestead by January 1, 2012. The SOH benefit can be transferred to a newly acquired residence anywhere in the state of Florida and is calculated differently, depending on whether the purchase price of the new residence is greater (upsizing) or less (downsizing) than the selling price of the current residence. The transferred SOH benefits also apply to school taxes on the new homestead.

"Upsizing"

If "upsizing" to a home of equal or greater just value, the homestead owner can transfer 100 percent of the SOH benefit to the new homestead, up to a $500,000 transferred benefit. For example, suppose a homeowner sells a home for $400,000 that has an assessed value of $250,000. The accumulated SOH benefit is the difference, $400,000 - $250,000 or $150,000. If the homeowner purchases a new home for $500,000 (upsizing) then the entire SOH benefit can be applied so that the assessed value of the newly acquired residence is now $350,000 ($500,000 - $150,000).

"Downsizing"

If "downsizing" to a home with a lower just value, the homestead owner can transfer a SOH benefit that protects the same percentage of value of the new home as it did the former homestead, up to a $500,000 benefit. In the example above, suppose the homeowner downsized to a home purchased for $300,000. The new market value of $300,000 divided by the old market value of $400,000 is 75 percent. Thus, only $112,000 (75 percent of the original SOH benefit of $150,000) can be transferred to the new home. This would reduce the assessed value to $187,500 ($300,000 - $112,500).

Split Ownership

If two or more people own multiple homesteads and are moving into only one new homestead, they can transfer a benefit from one of the former homesteads up to a maximum of $500,000 of benefit.

If two or more people jointly own a homestead and are moving into more than one homestead, they must divide the value of their SOH benefit among the new homesteads based on the number of owners of the prior homestead. The total amount of transferable benefits is capped at $500,000.

PORTABILITY OF ACCUMULATED SOH BENEFIT

House Sold

Selling Price
$400,000

Fair Market Value:
$400,000

SOH Exempt Benefit:
$150,000

Capped Assessed Value:
$250,000

(Upsizing)
House Purchased

Purchase Price
$500,000

Fair Market Value:
$500,000

Applied SOH Exempt
Benefit (100%):
$150,000

New Home Assessed Value:
$350,000

(Downsizing)
House Purchased

Purchase Price
$300,000

Fair Market Value:
$300,000

Applied SOH Exempt
* Benefit (75%):
$112,500

New Home Assessed Value:
$187,500

$$ * \frac{\text{Market Value of New Home}}{\text{Market Value of Prior Home}} = 75\% $$

Change of Ownership

Notwithstanding the provisions of the Florida Constitutional SOH amendment discussed previously, anytime a Florida home undergoes a change of ownership, a reassessment may be required to determine the fair market value as of January 1 of the year following the change. That could present a trap for the unwary. Florida statute defines a "change of ownership" to include any sale, foreclosure or transfer of legal or beneficial title to any person. However, exceptions include transfers between spouses, between legal and equitable title, and after the change of ownership if the same person is entitled to the homestead exemption as was previously entitled (e.g., transferring the homestead to your revocable living trust).

The addition of a family member to the deed of a homestead property (e.g., a mother adding a daughter to the title) is not covered by the above exemptions and, thus, the tax clock would reset and start ticking all over again. Likewise, the transfer of a homestead to certain irrevocable trusts could cause a problem.

For example, transferring your home to a qualified personal residence trust (see Chapter 4), where title to the home passes to one or more of your children after a term of years has elapsed, may cause a reassessment at the end of the term of the trust, even if you continue to live in the home. With proper legal advice you may be able to avoid these potential traps and retain your exemption.

Homestead Protections

Subject to the discussion about federal law below, your Florida homestead provides a constitutional protection from creditors. It means that, in general, your home cannot be sold against your will to satisfy the claims of your creditors. Homestead protection extends to the full value of your home and up to one-half acre of land within city limits and 160 contiguous acres outside a municipality. The protection from creditors is found in Article X, Section 4, of the Florida Constitution, which reads, in part:

THE FLORIDA BLUEPRINT

Total area: 58,560 square miles (land and water)

Land area: 54,252 square miles

Total water area: 4,308 square miles

Rank among states in total area: 22nd

Length north to south: 447 miles

Width east to west: 361 miles

Distance from Pensacola to Key West: 792 miles by road

Highest natural point: 345 feet near Lakewood in Walton County

Geographic center: 12 miles northwest of Brooksville in Hernando County

Coastline: 1,197 miles

Tidal shoreline: 2,276 miles

Beaches: 663 miles

Rivers, streams and waterways: Over 11,000 miles

Longest river: St. Johns, 273 miles

Largest lake: Lake Okeechobee at 700 square miles; Lake Okeechobee is the second largest freshwater lake in the United States

Largest county: Palm Beach at 2,578 square miles

Smallest county: Union at 245 square miles

Number of lakes greater than 10 acres: Approximately 7,700

Number of first-magnitude springs: 33; more first-magnitude springs than any other state

Number of islands greater than 10 acres: Approximately 4,500; only Alaska has more

Source: myflorida.com.

There shall be exempt from forced sale under process of any court, and no judgment, decree or execution shall be a lien thereon, except for the payment of taxes and assessments thereon, obligations contracted for the purchase, improvement or repair thereof, or obligations contracted for house, field or other labor performed on the realty, the following property owned by a natural person: (1) A homestead, ...

The Florida Supreme Court has been very protective of homestead property. In only very limited circumstances has the Court allowed a creditor to reach a homestead, such as permitting an equitable lien where funds obtained through fraud or other wrongful conduct could be traced directly to investment in the homestead. However, the Florida Supreme Court specifically ruled that transfer of nonexempt assets into an exempt homestead, even with the intent to hinder, delay or defraud creditors, does not allow a creditor to overcome the exemption and impose a lien on homestead property.

Furthermore, the courts in Florida have been very generous in preventing forced sales of all sorts of home ownership, such as cooperative apartments, certain types of mobile homes or motor coaches and even some types of house boats.

In most cases the homestead protection (from the homeowner's creditors) passes to the surviving spouse or heirs of the owner. This protection can be a significant benefit to families if the homestead owner had substantial medical bills prior to death or if the deceased owner was involved in an accident for which the estate might be exposed to liability. Note two important points: (1) that the owner's homestead exemption protects the home against the owner's creditors, not the creditors of the surviving spouse or heirs and (2) this extension of protection against the owner's creditors to the owner's spouse and heirs does not apply to residences that cannot be ordinarily treated as interests in real estate, such as cooperative apartments and mobile homes.

Homestead and Federal Law

Although Florida is very generous with its homestead asset protection laws, it is not always clear that the protection will apply when the creditor involved is the federal government or a creditor's claim is made in federal bankruptcy court. For example, a Florida homestead is not exempt from federal tax liens.

Furthermore, because of the Bankruptcy Abuse Prevention and Consumer Protection Act of 2005, newcomers to Florida will find that their home may not qualify for full protection right away if they are involved in a bankruptcy and have not resided in Florida for 1,215 days (approximately three years and four months) prior to filing a bankruptcy petition. Under the new law, the homestead exemption is limited to $125,000 of equity if your homestead was acquired less than 1,215 days prior to a bankruptcy filing. This is true unless the homestead was acquired through an exempt rollover of proceeds from a prior exempt Florida residence and the combined holding period for the new and old exempt residences is 1,215 days. However, after the waiting period, Florida's unlimited exemption amount on your homestead will apply.

The 2005 bankruptcy law also contains provisions designed to prevent the conversion of nonexempt assets into exempt homestead property if such conversion is done with the intent to hinder, delay or defraud creditors. In such a case, the value of the homestead is reduced by the value of such converted property if the conversion took place during the ten-year period preceding the filing of bankruptcy. This includes a substantial reduction in any outstanding mortgage to avoid current or reasonably foreseeable creditors. Moreover, none of the homestead is exempt if the debtor is convicted of a felony in conjunction with an abusive filing (as determined by the bankruptcy court) or the debtor owes a debt related to any of the following:

- A violation of federal or state securities laws,

- The purchase of registered securities through fraud, deceit or manipulation or
- Any criminal act, intentional tort or willful or reckless misconduct that caused serious physical injury or death in the proceeding five years.

There is an exception to the complete nonexemption of the homestead of a debtor if the home is "reasonably necessary for the support of the debtor and any dependent." In this case, the exemption would be $125,000 of equity in the homestead.

Total Exemption of Homestead from Taxation

Real estate used and owned as a homestead by a quadriplegic, paraplegic or other totally and permanently disabled person who must use a wheelchair for mobility, or is legally blind, is exempt from ad valorem (real estate) taxation. The applicant must produce a certificate of this disability from two unrelated and professionally licensed Florida physicians. Except for quadriplegics, who are

FLORIDA'S SPIRIT FLIES

Florida's flag became official in 1900. Florida's flag has a diagonal red cross on a white field with the state seal in the center. The flag is based on the Confederate battle flag, which in turn was inspired by the cross of St. Andrew. The seal in the center illustrates a Seminole woman scattering flowers, the sun with many rays, palm trees, a sailing steamboat, and the land and the water.

Reprinted with permission of BigStockPhoto

Source: www.worldflags101.com

exempt, the income of all persons residing at the homestead (including Social Security benefits) cannot exceed an income ceiling determined yearly by the Florida Department of Revenue.

Further, real estate used and owned as a homestead by an American veteran—honorably discharged with a service-connected medical condition that resulted in total, permanent disability—is exempt from ad valorem taxation. The applicant must have a letter from the U.S. government or U.S. Department of Veteran Affairs confirming the disability. The veteran must be a permanent resident of Florida prior to January 1 of the tax year for which the exemption is being claimed.

For details, call the property appraiser's office for the county in which you are considering a new home. A list of all Florida county property appraisers, including contact information, can be found online at http://dor.myflorida.com/dor/property/appraisers.html.

Protection for a Spouse and Children

If you claim a Florida homestead, Florida law gives your spouse and minor children a special right in the home against your attempt to convey or encumber that home. Thus, even if the home is purchased in the sole name of a husband or wife (or a revocable living trust established by a husband or wife), when the home is mortgaged or resold, the lender or buyer will require one of the following:

- The signature of the other spouse on the mortgage, deed and/or conveying documents;
- A written waiver of homestead rights by the other spouse;
- A statement on the deed confirming the property is not the homestead of the person signing the conveying document so there is no question of a violation of a spouse's homestead rights and, therefore, no potential cloud on the title.

For estate planning purposes, the homestead residence in Florida may be the most difficult asset to transfer freely. The general rule is that when a homestead is owned solely by one spouse and that spouse dies, the surviving spouse obtains a "legal life estate" (the right to possess and use the home for the remainder of his or her life), with a remainder interest going to the owner's lineal descendants.

Specifically, Article X, Section 4(c), of the Florida Constitution states:

The homestead shall not be subject to devise (transfer) if the owner is survived by a spouse or minor child, except the homestead may be devised to the owner's spouse if there be no minor child. The owner of homestead real estate, joined by the spouse if married, may alienate the homestead by mortgage, sale or gift and, if married, may by deed transfer the title to an estate by the entirety with the spouse ...

For example, assume you are married and currently live in a state other than Florida. You own a Florida home that you have used as your vacation home. In a will, you leave the Florida home to your children from a prior marriage. In this case, the Florida home is not your homestead and can be freely transferred. However, if you move into the Florida home, declare Florida as your domicile and your spouse does not waive homestead rights before your death, your spouse will have a life estate in the home and your children from your prior marriage will receive the home only upon your spouse's death, regardless of what your will says.

Loss of Homestead Exemption

The rental of an entire dwelling previously claimed to be a homestead for tax purposes constitutes abandonment of the dwelling as a homestead resulting in loss of the homestead exemption. Abandonment of a homestead after January 1 of any year does not affect the homestead exemption for tax purposes for that particular year.

HURRICANE HEADQUARTERS

The Atlantic hurricane season, which affects Florida, runs for six months, from June 1 to November 30. Local TV stations and newspapers provide hurricane tracking maps, preparedness guides, seminars and regular forecasts so it is easy to be prepared. The National Hurricane Center's Web site, www.nhc.noaa.gov, provides the very latest information if a storm should develop.

Florida's first Weather Bureau Station opened in Miami in 1911. The National Hurricane Center, also located in Miami, provides hurricane analysis to 24 countries.

In 2005, seven major hurricanes hit the continental U.S. in or around Florida. There was much speculation that global warming was ushering in a new era in high hurricane activity for the Florida region. Such dire predictions for future years were unfounded as no major hurricanes made landfall  in Florida since then. The table below shows that the frequency of hurricanes of category 3 or greater in the continental U.S. is erratic, making trends difficult to establish.

Time Period	Hurricanes of Category >3
1901-1920	11
1921-1940	13
1941-1960	18
1961-1980	10
1981-2000	10
2001-2008	11

Source: National Hurricane Center

When, Where and How to File for the Exemption

To qualify for the homestead exemption in a certain year, you must have legal and equitable title to the property and reside in the property as your primary residence as of January 1; that is, you must have established your Florida domicile by January 1. Furthermore, you must apply in person (or by mail, if permitted in your county) prior to March 1 at the county appraiser's office or one of the satellite locations designated by the county appraiser throughout the county in which the property is located. The schedule indicating the satellite locations for filing for the exemption is usually published each year in the local newspaper or you may call the property appraiser's office in the county where your home is located for information.

If you were unable to establish title to your property by the first of January, you will not qualify for the homestead exemption in that particular year; thus, you will have to wait until the following

FLORIDA'S UNIQUE SUBTROPICAL CLIMATE

New residents may find it difficult to detect the subtle changes in seasons from spring to summer to fall, but there are other seasons in Florida that are immediately recognizable. Most apparent are the rainy and dry seasons. Summer rainstorms begin in late May and continue through October.

Average summer precipitation (August) is about 8 inches, while average winter precipitation (January) is approximately 3 inches.

The Gulf of Mexico's average water temperature ranges from the low to mid-60s from January through March and in the 80s from June through September. On the east coast, Atlantic Ocean temperatures are consistently a few degrees cooler.

Source: visitflorida.com; NOAA; and Florida Climate Center.

year to establish your homestead exemption. However, most Florida county offices accept pre-filed applications for the following tax year throughout the current year so that you might avoid long lines at the regular filing times.

You must produce certain documents, dated prior to January 1 of the tax year for which you are applying for the exemption, to verify your qualification for the exemption. These documents typically include the following:

- A copy of your declaration of domicile that was filed with the clerk of the circuit court;
- A recorded deed or copy of the tax bill to your Florida home in your name—as evidence of ownership;
- Social Security numbers for all owners (i.e., for you and your spouse if the home is in both your names);
- Your Florida driver license. If you don't drive, you must show a highway patrol ID card issued by the Florida Division of Driver Licenses;
- Your Florida vehicle registration;
- Your Voter's registration card for the county in which your home is located;
- Your resident alien "green" card if you are not a U.S. citizen;
- A complete copy of the trust agreement—so that eligibility of the trust to qualify for the homestead exemption can be determined if your property is held in a trust.

A sample application for homestead exemption (Form DR 501) is included in Appendix B2.

It's not what you gather in life, but what you scatter in life that tells the kind of life you've lived and the kind of person you are.
— **Helen Walton**

CHAPTER 4

ESTATE PLANNING FOR FLORIDA RESIDENTS

As discussed in Chapter 2, Florida has no separate state income tax, gift tax or estate tax, and is unlikely to have any of these taxes in the foreseeable future. The Economic Growth and Tax Relief Reconciliation Act of 2001 eliminated a mechanism by which the federal government shared estate tax revenues with the states. This sharing arrangement was often referred to by the states as the state "sponge" tax or "pickup" tax.

A number of states, in response to this loss of revenue, have "decoupled" from the old sharing arrangement and have enacted separate state estate or inheritance taxes. Florida has not decoupled! In fact, based on a strict reading, the State Constitution prohibits decoupling. Hence, Florida's Constitution prevents the enactment of a separate state estate tax, absent a change to the Constitution by the voters of Florida.

Estate Tax Exposure on Non-Florida Real Estate

The absence of estate, gift or generation-skipping transfer (GST) tax in Florida is good news if you are planning on becoming a permanent Florida resident. However, if after you become a Florida resident and you still own property (typically, real estate) in your former state at your death, there may be ramifications if that state has decoupled from the federal estate tax system and established a separate estate tax. Depending on the value of your property in another state, it is possible that your former state will want to tax your property at your death—even if no federal estate tax is due.

Some decoupled states have set a level of exemption from their state estate tax that is well below the federal estate tax exemption. For example, in New Jersey, the state exemption is currently only $675,000. So, if you own real estate in New Jersey at the time of your death with a value in excess of the state exemption amount, the state will assess a tax on your estate. Furthermore, it may not matter if you are married. Even if you die first and pass all or a portion of that real estate to your spouse in a typical bypass ("B") trust designed to use your federal estate tax exemption while benefiting your spouse and family, the trust may not protect your estate from state estate tax.

WHAT'S A CONCH?

Florida's state shell is the horse conch, a mollusk with a large pale orange shell. Though today the shellfish is rare, there are many conchs on dry land. "Conch" is a term used today to indicate a native of the Keys, especially Key West. Originally, though, it described Bahamians of European descent. One of the theories on the origin of the term is that the Europeans ate a great deal of conch. However it originated, the term evolved to include Europeans in the Florida Keys and the name stuck.

Reprinted with permission of BigStockPhoto

Source: The Florida Keys: A History of the Pioneers by John Viele.

Fundamental Estate Planning

For a well-planned estate—one that avoids probate, takes care of you in the event of your incapacity and helps confirm your status as a Florida resident—you should have the following basic estate planning documents:

- Living will
- Health care surrogate designation
- Health Insurance Portability and Accountability Act (HIPAA) authorization for release of medical information
- Revocable living trust
- Pour-over will
- Power of attorney

Living Will

A living will is a document in which you state whether or not life-sustaining procedures should be used to prolong your life if you are terminally ill, you have an end-stage condition, or you are in a persistent vegetative state. Florida, like most states, has specifically approved the use of living wills by statute.

With modern medical technology improving every day, the possibility of prolonging life can go far beyond what most people have ever imagined. Yet many people are unwilling to suffer the loss of their dignity—and possibly their life savings, as the necessary payment for prolonging their lives—when death is otherwise imminent. They simply want to retain the right to control decisions regarding their medical care, including the withholding or withdrawing of life-sustaining procedures.

Florida's living will laws contain safeguards to ensure peace of mind, such as a requirement that two physicians examine the patient and determine that recovery is no longer likely before life-sustaining treatments may be withdrawn. If you sign a living will, you can revoke it at any time by destroying it, directing its destruction or by signing a written revocation.

DESTINATION THEME PARK

In the 1960s, Walt Disney came to Florida in search of a site for a model idealized working community. On October 1, 1971, Walt Disney World opened and was followed soon after by EPCOT (an acronym for his Experimental Prototype City of Tomorrow). This subsequently expanded into a larger network of theme parks, resort hotels and communities that now exist on the Disney property.

When President Kennedy launched the space program, NASA laid claim to a huge parcel of land on the northeast coast for the John F. Kennedy Space Center. The center offers IMAX theaters, the Astronaut Hall of Fame, museums devoted to space exploration and space simulation rides. See more about the Kennedy Space Center on page 99.

Busch Entertainment Corp., the family entertainment division of Anheuser-Busch, runs Sea World and Busch Gardens. Busch Gardens, located in Tampa, opened in 1959 as an African theme park. You can explore African wildlife, along with many roller coasters. This park also features the famous Budweiser Clydesdales. Sea World, located in Orlando, opened in 1973 as a fun park featuring many sea creatures.

NASCAR fans will enjoy a live test-drive experience at the Richard Petty Driving Experience. Featured at three locations, Miami, Orlando and Daytona, you can experience the real life thrill of riding with a driver at 165 miles per hour.

Created in 1946, Weeki Wachee Springs is a water park that will supply fun for the whole family. This park was built on a spring in Brooksville and features Buccaneer Bay water park, canoe and glass bottom boat rides, snorkeling, scuba diving and an underwater theater with mermaid shows.

Source: visitflorida.com.

Health Care Surrogate Designation

A designation of health care surrogate is a document, authorized under Florida laws, that allows you to chose a person to make your medical decisions for you if you cannot. It covers decisions on issues that may arise before you are terminally ill, such as operations, transfusions, nursing care and various medical treatments. Florida law has the effect of empowering your agent to make virtually any type of health care decision you could make for yourself.

Release of Medical Information

The Health Insurance Portability and Accountability Act (HIPAA) authorization for release of information helps ensure your agent (i.e., a family member) will have the right to obtain your medical records to share with health care professionals should the need arise. The HIPAA authorization can be a separate document or can be incorporated in other documents, such as your health care surrogate designation.

Revocable Living Trust

Whether you die in Florida or elsewhere, you should have a proper estate plan that includes instructions on how you want your assets distributed at death. This could be accomplished with a will, but it is often better accomplished through the use of a revocable living trust (RLT).

A will is only operative at your death, whereas an RLT goes far beyond a will by providing instructions about how you want your affairs to be handled while you are alive and well or if you become incapacitated. Your RLT includes instructions on how you would like your property and financial affairs managed and it forms the foundation of an effective estate plan.

In most RLTs, you, as the trust maker (or "grantor"), are the trustee of your trust during your lifetime. As trustee, you continue to manage your assets and file your federal income tax returns as you always have. In addition, you may transfer assets to and from the trust whenever you desire. You can name your spouse as co-trustee or as a "successor" trustee, the person who would take over if you resign, become disabled or die.

An RLT offers two major benefits to you and your family that cannot be achieved with a will:

- Avoidance of probate and
- Protection in the event of your incapacity

Avoiding Probate

The most talked about advantage of an RLT is the avoidance of probate. Many people mistakenly think that they avoid probate by having a will. Just the opposite is true. Relying on a will to dispose of assets guarantees probate because the purpose of probate is to prove the validity of the will. A properly drafted RLT that is funded with your assets during your lifetime, on the other hand, can minimize or even avoid probate. There are numerous reasons why it is best to avoid probate, even in Florida where the probate process is considered to be fairly simple. Following are some of those reasons:

FRIENDS FROM ABROAD

With a mild climate and gorgeous beaches, Florida continues to be a hot spot for vacationers from all over the world. And despite bad press over the threat of oil-soaked beaches, tourism to Florida was up for the second quarter of 2010. In fact, U.S. residents vacationing in Florida is up 2.4 percent and overseas tourism is up 11.9 percent, with a 10.4 percent increase in travelers from Canada.

Source: www.visitflorida.com

Cost: The costs associated with probating your estate, including attorney fees, court costs, appraisals and so on, range from three to 15 percent of the gross estate, depending on the state in which you are domiciled at your death. The cost of preparing a typical RLT is usually very small in comparison to the costs of probating your estate—which would be the result of dying with only a will. If properly funded, an RLT can completely avoid probate and the associated costs.

Time: Probate takes time and it can easily be a year or more before the process is completed. In the absence of tax issues, with an RLT, there is virtually no waiting because the trust does not die; only the grantor does.

State lines: Wills do not cross state lines well. If you have property, such as real estate, in more than one state, your heirs will likely face "ancillary" probate in each additional state where your property is located. This can add to the costs and time delays. With a properly funded RLT, probate is often unnecessary, regardless of where the properties are located.

Public: Wills are public records. An RLT is private; virtually nothing will be known by the public about your estate and the details of the inheritance your heirs receive.

Contests: Wills are often easier than trusts to contest. You may believe that your heirs won't challenge your will but, when people die, heirs may begin quarreling among each other. You cannot be sure that no one will contest your wishes. As a client once remarked, "If you really want to get to know someone, share an inheritance with that person." An RLT is harder to dispute because it is a "living" document and usually funded by you before you die. Also, with you as trustee of your RLT, there leaves little doubt about your true intentions. With an RLT, typically, you may make any changes you desire while you are alive and competent. If an heir believes he or she has a basis for a lawsuit, the heir would have to bring suit themselves rather than simply raising the issue in an already-established probate proceeding.

Providing for Disability

The second major reason for having an RLT, and one that many experts consider more important than avoiding probate, is having your wishes carried out in the event you become incapacitated. The fact is you are four to six times more likely to become disabled than to die in the next year. Therefore, it is important to be prepared so that you and your loved ones can be cared for in the manner you desire during your incapacity.

Many people feel that they have adequately planned for incapacity because they have a durable power of attorney. A durable power of attorney is a legal document that gives the person of your choice the right to act in your place regarding all financial matters. Unfortunately, some financial institutions won't recognize a durable power of attorney, especially if the document is old and does not contain language dictated by state law. Even though Florida has a law that requires a financial institution to honor a durable power of attorney, if the document is not drafted in accordance with the Florida statute, problems may arise.

An RLT, on the other hand, allows you to choose, in detail, how you want your affairs handled if you become incapacitated and lets you set the priority of your wishes. Financial institutions are more likely to recognize and follow RLT instructions when the grantor of the trust is disabled or incapacitated.

If you have neither a durable power of attorney nor an RLT and you become incapacitated, your spouse or your children would have to go through the legal process of guardianship. And although the probate court would most likely appoint your spouse (or adult family member if you have no spouse) to manage your affairs, he or she would have to report annually to the court and your affairs would be subject to legal costs and the red tape of the court system. Fortunately, this can all be easily avoided with an RLT; your successor trustee (typically your spouse) manages your affairs beginning the moment you become disabled without any legal proceedings or court intervention.

Planning for Estate Taxes

An RLT can provide you with benefits you cannot receive with a will and typically includes your instructions for minimizing federal estate taxes. A married person who leaves everything to his or her spouse in what is known as an "I love you" will avoids any federal estate tax at the death of the first spouse because of the unlimited federal marital deduction (no tax on assets left to your spouse). However, at the surviving spouse's death, the property owned by that spouse, including the property inherited from the first spouse to die, is then subjected to the federal estate tax. The problem with this simple arrangement is that it wastes the "applicable exclusion amount" of the first spouse to die. With a properly worded RLT, it is possible to preserve your exemption by leaving the exemption amount either directly to others (e.g., your children) or to a trust that is set up to benefit your family, including your spouse.

A common arrangement involves the use of an RLT that splits into two trusts upon the first death: a marital trust (also known as a qualified terminable interest property (QTIP) trust or the "A" trust) and a family trust (often referred to as a bypass trust, a credit shelter trust or simply a "B" trust). The family trust preserves the applicable exclusion amount of the first spouse to die while providing for the needs of the surviving spouse, while the marital trust preserves the unlimited marital deduction for the balance of the estate.

SNOW BIRDS

Common brown pelicans remain in Florida all year. The endangered white pelicans, like many of our seasonal residents, are sometimes referred to as "snow birds" because they arrive in Florida during the cold northern winter months and return to their northern homes for the spring and summer.

Reprinted with permission of BigStockPhoto

Protecting Your Heirs

An RLT also offers flexibility in regard to how you leave your assets to help protect your heirs. You may, for example, pass assets to your heirs with "strings attached." By doing so, you can control how and when your assets are to be distributed after your death.

For example, one new Florida resident had a son who was a "deadhead" (i.e., a follower of the rock group known as the Grateful Dead). The son would follow the group from concert to concert and sell tie-dyed T-shirts to make enough money to eat and travel. The parents were quite wealthy but were worried about their son's lifestyle and propensity for spending money. So in their RLT, they arranged for their son to receive his inheritance through a trust that provided him with two dollars from their estate for every dollar he legitimately earned. This type of trust is commonly referred to as an "incentive trust."

Many professional planners believe that no one should leave anything of any consequence to anyone outright. Instead, everything should be left in "asset protection" trusts. By leaving assets in trust for children, you can protect them in a way they cannot do for themselves.

THE CITRUS SIDE OF FLORIDA

Florida has a long and profitable history of orange juice production that began during World War II when concentrated juice was invented. The process removed the water from the juice so it could be stored and re-hydrated later. The industry really took off with frozen concentrate and now it's a multibillion dollar industry. Most Florida oranges are grown in the southern two-thirds of the state, out of the reach of frosts. The height of the season is December through May, when a trip to a local fruit stand will yield fresh oranges and a variety of other succulent citrus.

Source: myflorida.com; floridajuice.com.

For example, your RLT could provide for each child to receive his or her inheritance in trust, allowing the child to serve as his or her own trustee or as a co-trustee. As a trustee, each child, or, for that matter, any of your heirs, can manage the funds however he or she desires. However, by retaining everything in trust, you may successfully prevent an unwanted creditor from a failed business venture, an overzealous litigator (e.g., as a result of an auto accident) or even a child's spouse or ex-spouse from ever gaining access to the assets in the trust.

In essence, you may accomplish two very important goals: you will have (1) set the assets aside, allowing each child to manage and benefit from his or her own share and (2) preserved the assets from successful attack by a third party.

When offered the opportunity to provide asset protection for their children, parents are sometimes concerned that by leaving assets in trust they are overcontrolling their children. This is a legitimate concern that must be reviewed with a qualified attorney. Keeping assets in trust for children should never be a question if the children can serve as trustees. This arrangement will provide them with significant flexibility and control. This simple arrangement should be compared with a more elaborate design involving co-trustees or "independent" trustees. Though more complicated, the latter arrangement arguably provides more protection from creditors, etc., than the former.

Another issue you would need to face is whether to allow your children to leave the assets remaining in their respective trusts to anyone they desire at their deaths (for example, to their spouses—who might remarry and choose to disinherit your grandchildren) or whether to restrict them to leaving these assets to your descendants.

Furthermore, by including generation-skipping provisions in your RLT (though you do not really skip anyone, except the IRS), you can also protect your children and grandchildren from additional layers of estate tax on a substantial portion of the assets that remain in trust at death. This protection can last up to 360 years in Florida. However, there is a limit on how much you can leave in trust that "skips" the IRS.

In summary, the RLT is a very flexible tool that will allow you to remain in control of your estate while providing a way to avoid probate, follow your wishes in the event of your disability, help save estate taxes, protect your heirs and avoid additional estate taxes at your children's deaths.

Funding Your RLT

To obtain the full benefits of having an RLT, it should be "funded" with virtually all your assets, with the notable exception of any qualified retirement plan assets, such as an IRA, 401(k), annuities and, possibly, your Florida home. Funding involves the transfer of assets from your name to your name as trustee (or to some other trustee, if appropriate) of your RLT.

GEOGRAPHY: CENTRAL FLORIDA

Central Florida stretches from Gainesville to Lake Okeechobee. Some of the major cities included in central Florida are Orlando, Lakeland, Ocala and Gainesville. Central Florida has few beaches, but hundreds of freshwater lakes that provide excellent bass fishing and freshwater springs, such as those showcased at Silver Springs. Horse lovers are sure to enjoy the rolling hills around Ocala where thoroughbred racehorses are raised. For urban pleasures, Orlando has a thriving nightlife scene and families flock to its many theme parks, including Disney World, Universal Studios and Sea World. Finally, Gainesville, home of the University of Florida Gators, offers a funky college town experience.

FACTS ABOUT CENTRAL FLORIDA

Orlando attracts more visitors than any other amusement park destination in the United States.

Gatorade was named for the University of Florida Gators where the drink was first developed.

Aviator Tony Jannus made history on January 1, 1914, when he flew the world's first scheduled passenger airline flight from St. Petersburg's downtown yacht basin to Tampa.

Neil Smith and his brother of Montverde developed the first Snapper riding lawn mower.

Plant City, the Winter Strawberry Capital of the World, holds the Guinness record for the world's largest strawberry shortcake. The 827 square foot, 6,000 pound cake was made on February 19, 1999, in McCall Park.

Fort Meade is the oldest settlement in Polk County. It dates back to 1849 when a settlement grew around the U.S. Calvary fort during the Seminole Indian Wars.

The Fred Bear Museum in Gainesville is a tribute to the accomplishments of Fred Bear, a promoter of proper wildlife management and the founder of Bear Archery Company.

The Hawthorne Trail, a part of Florida's Rails to Trails program, attracts many outdoor enthusiasts to walk, cycle or ride horseback through its 17-mile length.

The Pinellas Trail, a 47-mile hiking/biking trail connecting St. Petersburg with central and north Pinellas County, is the longest urban linear trail in the eastern United States.

An annuity, IRA or typical qualified plan has its own beneficiary designation form and, therefore, would not be controlled by your will or trust unless one or more of those instruments names your trust as the beneficiary at your death. Also, by changing the ownership of a qualified plan, IRA or annuity to your trust, you may unnecessarily trigger income tax.

You should seek legal advice on whether to title your Florida homestead residence in your RLT, as you may lose valuable protection against creditors. In a case decided a few years ago by a federal bankruptcy court for the Middle District of Florida, the judge

FLORIDA PARKS & MONUMENTS

Florida contains 160 state parks existing on more than 700,000 acres. The parks feature crystal-clear springs, miles of beaches, rivers, lakes and an abundance of wildlife and outdoor activities. Also, there are 33

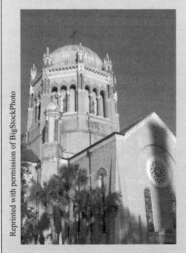

state forests and seven park preserves in Florida. Five national monuments and memorials show Florida's history: Castillo de San Marcos, DeSoto, Fort Caroline, Fort Jefferson and Fort Matanzas. The architecture in these historic sites reveals the rich diversity of Florida's first European settlers.

After a colorful history of occupation by the British and then re-occupation by the Spanish, the oldest city in the United States, St. Augustine, and the entire state of Florida, was sold to America in 1821. In 1883, oil baron Henry Flagler restored St. Augustine and turned it into a winter resort.

Reprinted with permission of BigStockPhoto

Source: www.visitflorida.org

determined that the creditor exemption under Florida's Constitution for a homestead residence does not apply when the residence is held in an RLT. The reasoning behind the ruling was that a revocable living trust is not considered a "natural person" as defined in the Florida Constitution and, therefore, does not meet the requirement under the Constitution that a homestead be owned by a natural person. Although this position has since been rejected by a number of courts (including two federal bankruptcy courts), prudence suggests that you should consult with a qualified estate planning attorney before transferring your homestead to an RLT.

Pour-Over Will

One of the most common mistakes in estate planning is failing to fund an RLT. Any asset that has not been placed in your name as trustee of your RLT will be subject to probate and, perhaps, guardianship. To ensure that all your assets end up in your trust containing your detailed instructions on the disposition of your assets at death, your attorney should arrange for you to execute a will that directs any assets not in your RLT to "pour over" into the trust. This is known as a pour-over will.

Special Durable Power of Attorney for Funding

A durable power of attorney is a document that allows you, as principal, to authorize another person (the "attorney" or agent) to act on your behalf with respect to specified legal matters, even if you subsequently become incapacitated. This document names who will make decisions and lists the decision-making powers it confers. A special durable power of attorney for funding limits your agent's authority to the funding of assets into your revocable living trust and would typically be used in the event of your incapacity.

Life Insurance

Life insurance is a legal contract, referred to as a policy, that guarantees to pay a certain sum of money (the death benefit) to a specified person or entity (the beneficiary) when the insured dies. The policy remains in effect as long as the cost of it (the premium) has been paid according to the contractual provisions.

You can own a policy personally or have some other person or entity, such as a trust, own it instead. The owner controls the policy and has the legal right to name the beneficiary, change the beneficiary, cancel the policy and/or withdraw or borrow from the policy's cash value at any time. The owner is responsible for any tax consequences relating to the premium, cash value and death benefit.

Most people don't think of it this way, but life insurance is risk sharing among a group of people with the common goal of providing money to beneficiaries when an insured party dies. It is somewhat like a lottery in that money is pooled to provide a benefit (death benefit) which, in the case of life insurance, goes to the beneficiaries of those who die while their contract is in force. Most Floridians purchase insurance because they love someone or something, but life insurance can be used for many purposes, such as:

- Providing financial security for loved ones.
- Protecting future generations.
- Paying estate taxes.
- Replacing wealth.
- Paying a debt, such as a mortgage.
- Equalizing inheritance.
- Purchasing an interest in a business.
- Protecting a business.
- Diversifying an investment portfolio.
- Giving to charity.
- Providing for retirement.
- Replacing lost income.
- Offsetting gifts to charity.
- Making up for a bad investment.
- Recovering the cost of a corporate obligation.

Life insurance is often the only way to effectively provide for many of the above needs. In most cases, it is the least expensive way. Life insurance is so versatile that it can provide benefits during life as well as after death. For example, in certain types of life insurance there is an accumulation of cash inside the policy from premium payments paid in excess of mortality charges and expenses. The policy owner can access this accumulation during his or her lifetime via withdrawals and/or policy loans. These withdrawals and loans are often tax-deferred and, if the policy is held to maturity, can be tax-free—allowing the full amount to be used for lifetime needs, such as retirement income, college educations and emergencies.

Life Settlement

If a life insurance policy is no longer needed or wanted, the policy can be "cashed in" to the insurance company for its current cash value, if any, or it can be sold in what is known as a life settlement transaction. The sale of insurance policies through a life settlement is a relatively new and fast-growing industry. Life settlement companies, often backed by hedge funds, pension funds and, in some cases, well-known financial institutions, act as "funders" and purchase policies for more than their current cash surrender value. The proceeds from a life settlement can be used for any number of purposes, including:

- To fund alternative financial products.
- To pay off medical bills.
- To offset increased living expenses.
- To make gifts to family members.
- To purchase a vacation home.
- To buy a replacement policy with the same death benefit but lower premiums.
- To buy a replacement policy with better guarantees.
- To buy a replacement policy with the same premium but a larger death benefit.

Virtually any type of policy from any carrier—including individual term (if the policy is convertible), whole and universal life, group, corporate-owned and policies held in irrevocable trusts—can be sold for more than the current cash value, for some percentage of the death benefit. The most attractive settlements are for policies with a death benefit of $500,000 or more where the insured is over 65 years of age and has had a health change since the policy was issued. However, an insured does not have to be sick to qualify for a life settlement.

Whatever your reason for terminating an existing policy, before you let your life insurance policy lapse or settle for the cash surrender value, you should check to see if a life settlement company will offer a better alternative. You can learn more about life insurance and life settlements for Florida residents online at www.fldfs.com and/or www.kilbournassociates.com.

FLORIDA DINOSAURS

Alligators, these iconic reptiles, have made a remarkable comeback from the endangered species list and now they are thriving in all sixty-seven Florida counties. In fact, they are so plentiful that the Florida Fish and Wildlife Conservation Commission removes about 5,000 nuisance gators each year and issues a certain number of permits each year to control the population. It is illegal to feed or harass the alligators. At up to 14 feet in length and 1,000 pounds in weight, a mature alligator can be an awe-inspiring sight.

Reprinted with permission BigStockPhoto.com

Source: myfwc.com.

Asset Protection Planning

Proper planning includes protecting your assets from unjust and unduly large judgments obtained by creditors. It is a prudent and, in some cases, necessary course of action, especially if you are wealthy—a characteristic that frequently makes people the target of gold-digging plaintiffs. By protecting your assets and reducing your liability exposure, potential plaintiffs are likely to either refrain from filing suit or settle early to save litigation costs and time.

Transferring your assets to a Revocable Living Trust (RLT) will not protect your assets from your creditors; however, there are several entities, often used in estate and wealth planning, that could help provide asset protection. Three of the most common are the family limited partnership, the family limited liability company and the irrevocable trust.

Family Limited Partnerships

A family limited partnership (FLP) is a business entity formed among family members under state law (i.e., Florida statutes). Individuals contribute property to the partnership in exchange for limited or general partnership interests. General partnership interests, no matter how small, control the management of and distributions from the partnership, while limited partnership interests are generally passive and only receive income, if earned, at the direction and under the control of the general partner. While the general partner is liable for debts of the partnership, limited partners are protected from claims of creditors because of the passive nature of the interests.

Owners of an FLP may enhance the asset protection benefits offered under Florida law by electing to form (or convert an existing FLP to) a limited liability limited partnership, which is a special form of limited partnership that limits the liability of not only the limited partners, but the general partner, as well.

In the context of estate planning, the biggest advantage of an FLP is that the fair market value of the limited partnership shares is typically less than the value of the underlying assets. This reflects the fact that limited partners don't have control and the interests are less marketable (often because of restrictions in the partnership agreement). Such "discounts" to the underlying value of the FLP can potentially allow FLP shares to be valued at as little as 50 percent of the underlying asset value, thereby reducing the base upon which gift or estate taxes are levied when the shares are given to loved ones during life or at death.

Family Limited Liability Companies

The family limited liability company (FLLC) is a type of hybrid business structure that is designed to provide the limited liability features of a corporation and the tax efficiencies and operational flexibility of a partnership. The FLLC is formed under state law among family members and is one of the easiest and least expensive forms of ownership to organize. It is a popular choice among families who are looking for asset protection and other benefits without the complication of a corporation.

Unlike an FLP where, under the laws of most states including Florida, the general partner (parents or other entity) is not protected from liability, all owners of the shares of an FLLC, including the "managing member(s)," have limited liability for business debts.

Parents can transfer FLLC ownership interests, often at discount (so that transfers can be made that are larger than their gift tax exemptions might otherwise allow), in the form of non-voting, non-manager interests, to children and/or grandchildren (or trusts for their benefit) without relinquishing control.

Estate Planning Benefits of an FLP or FLLC

In estate planning, a family limited partnership (FLP) or family limited liability company (FLLC) is often used to enhance an efficient wealth transfer program. The use of either entity could accomplish the following:

- Provide centralized asset management for family assets;
- Provide the opportunity for significant discounts to the fair market value of any gifts you make, allowing you to give more, possibly as much as 80 to 100 percent more than your gift tax exclusion would allow. The discounts (determined through appraisals) result from a "lack of marketability" and "lack of control" relative to the FLP or FLLC interests;
- Allow you to fund your FLP or FLLC with many types of assets, including stocks, bonds, real estate and cash;
- Allow you, as general partner of an FLP or managing member of an FLLC, to charge a "reasonable" management fee which provides you with the option of earning a portion of the income produced by assets in the FLP or FLLC—before distributions are made on a pro-rata basis;
- Allow the appreciation of assets owned by the FLP or FLLC, to the extent given to family members (or trusts for their benefit), to occur outside your estate—free of gift or estate tax;
- Provide a way to consolidate multistate family real estate in one entity to avoid ancillary probate and potential domicile claims by a former state of residence;
- Protect the assets placed inside the FLP or FLLC from attachment by individual creditors.

Irrevocable Trusts

A typical irrevocable trust (IRT) is a trust that you set up while you are alive for the benefit of others and that you normally cannot change. The trustee of an IRT is usually someone other than you (the "grantor") because the trust cannot be controlled by or benefit the grantor without the risk of having the value of the trust assets included in the grantor's estate for estate tax purposes. By transferring one or more assets to an IRT, you are making irrevocable gifts. Thus, if the IRT is properly worded, the assets owned by the IRT are out of the reach of your creditors and those of your trust beneficiaries—while the assets are in the trust. Below are four examples of IRTs, with a summary of the primary purpose of each.

Qualified Personal Residence Trusts

A qualified personal residence trust (QPRT) typically allows you to transfer one or more homes, after the passage of a specified period of time (while you continue to live in and use the home), to one or more family members or other heirs at a value less than the current market value. It involves discounting the value of your gift of the home based on the term (period of time) of the QPRT (e.g., 10 years) using the appropriate government-determined interest rate. This arrangement leads to a reduction in the amount of exemption used or gift tax due—for making the gift. If you own a residence in a state that has decoupled from the federal estate tax system, a QPRT may provide the added benefit of eliminating your exposure to any state estate tax that might be due at your death (though, if you are domiciled in a state other than Florida, you may be subject to a current state gift tax in that state when you set the trust up). At the end of the term of the QPRT, the named beneficiaries (i.e., children or a trust for their benefit) will own the home.

Grantor Retained Annuity Trusts

A grantor retained annuity trust (GRAT) is a tax-efficient way to transfer appreciating assets to your heirs, after a stated period of time, while providing several benefits, including the following:

- Allows you to make gifts of property to your children or other heirs (or a trust for their benefit) while retaining an income interest in the property for a period of years;
- Reduces the gift tax value (possibly to zero) of the assets you give to the trust by delaying the actual enjoyment of the property by the beneficiaries for a period of years;
- Removes growth on the assets from your taxable estate, thereby eliminating any gift or estate taxes on the appreciation.

Irrevocable Life Insurance Trusts

The primary purpose of an irrevocable life insurance trust (ILIT) is to own a policy of insurance while protecting the cash value and the insurance proceeds from creditors and the IRS. Life insurance is often a very important financial tool in estate tax planning, as it creates needed liquidity for paying taxes and expenses as well as providing tax-free cash for beneficiaries. An ILIT can be designed

THE REAL FLORIDA NATIVES

At the end of the Great Ice Age, 12,000 years ago, the first Native Americans came into what is now Florida. By the time the Europeans arrived, there were hundreds of different Indian societies throughout the area of "La Florida."

From the Apalachee tribe in the northeastern panhandle to the Matecumbe in the Keys, Florida was the original home of the Tequesta, Calusa, Ocale, Potano, Timucua, Tocobaga, Ais, Jeaga and dozens of other groups. Because of the varied geography, the many Indian cultures adapted to their unusual surroundings.

Surviving and flourishing for thousands of years prior to the European "discovery" of Florida, these local Indians were virtually extinct by the middle of the 1800s–primarily as victims of warfare and disease.

Among the best known Indian tribes in Florida today are the Seminole and Miccosukee, many of whom descended from the Creek Indians of Alabama and Georgia. However, there are currently more than 125 other tribes identified in Florida, from Apache to Yurok, with the Cherokee as the largest tribe.

Source: Florida's Indians from Ancient Times to the Present by Jerald T. Milanich, 1998, University Press of Florida.

as a generation-skipping ("dynasty") trust and allow the insurance proceeds to benefit more than one generation of family members without the imposition of tax at each generation.

Charitable Remainder Trusts

A charitable remainder trust (CRT) is an irrevocable trust that allows you to make a charitable contribution and diversify your assets without paying immediate income tax while retaining an income stream. Grantors typically transfer property, usually appreciated stock or appreciated real estate, but other assets can also be contributed. The donor of the property typically designates himself or herself as trustee. The donor and spouse generally are the income beneficiaries of the CRT for their lifetimes. This allows the donor-beneficiary to retain control of and receive income from the contributed assets. Once transferred into the CRT, the assets are often free from the claims of creditors. Upon the death of the income beneficiaries, any assets left in the CRT are distributed to one or more charities designated by you as grantor.

Charitable Remainder Trust Benefits

A charitable remainder trust can accomplish the following:

- Allows you to avoid immediate capital gain tax on the sale of highly appreciated property (e.g., real estate, stocks/bonds);
- Allows you the option to remain in control of the assets contributed because you may be the trustee of your CRT;
- Provides a source of greater income for your life and, possibly, the lives of your spouse and other family members;
- Helps to diversify your assets;
- Provides an income tax deduction and resulting tax savings that may be invested to replace the contribution, possibly through the use of life insurance owned by an ILIT;
- Protects assets from the claims of creditors;
- Allows you to leave a legacy to your favorite charity or your own foundation at your death.

Asset Protection for Florida Residents

Your decision to become a resident of Florida entitles you to various protections under Florida law. Florida's asset protection laws are among the most liberal, debtor-friendly laws in the country. A Florida resident's personal property and intangible assets are covered by Florida's favorable asset protection laws regardless of where the accounts and assets are held. If a Florida resident's real property is located in another state, then the asset protection laws of that state apply to the real property. Here is a summary of many of the protections provided to you when you have declared Florida to be your domicile.

Homestead

As discussed in detail in Chapter 3, your Florida homestead—including the full value of your home and up to one-half acre of land in the city limits and 160 contiguous acres outside of a municipality—has constitutional protection from creditors. The protection is subject to provisions of the Bankruptcy Abuse Prevention and Consumer Protection Act of 2005.

Retirement Plans

Florida Statute § 222.21(2)(a) provides that any money or other assets payable to a participant or beneficiary in a qualified retirement plan—including a profit sharing plan, individual retirement account (IRA), Roth IRA, 401(k) plan and other tax qualified plans—is exempt from all claims of creditors of the beneficiary or participant.

In the case of IRAs and Roth IRA accounts, if a bankruptcy is involved, the amount exempted under the 2005 bankruptcy law is limited to $1 million unless the owner can demonstrate that the excess amount represents rollover distributions from one or more qualified retirement plans.

Life Insurance

Under Florida law, the death benefit and cash value of a life insurance policy for owners, insureds and beneficiaries are protected.

FLORIDA SEA TURTLES

Five species of protected sea turtles are found in Florida waters: the loggerhead, the green, the leatherback, the Kemp's Ridley and the hawksbill.

Loggerhead sea turtles are the most common species seen in Florida and the beaches along the Treasure Coast make up the most important loggerhead nesting site in the hemisphere. Females arrive every summer to nest. A female lays around one hundred eggs in a narrow pit she digs, usually in beach sand, with her hind flippers. Once she returns to the ocean, the hatchlings are on their own. If they are lucky, they will reach maturity in twenty-five to thirty-five years and return to the same beach where they were hatched to lay a new generation of eggs.

Reprinted with permission of BigStockPhoto

Beachfront residents know not to disturb the nests and to turn out their lights at night from May through October to avoid confusing sea turtle hatchlings, which rely on the starlight reflected from the ocean to find their way back to sea.

Source: www.myfwc.com

Death benefit: Insurance policy proceeds are exempt for any party (owner, insured or beneficiary) if payable to a named beneficiary other than the insured, insured's estate, executors, administrators or assigns.

Cash value: While a Florida resident is alive, the cash surrender value of any insurance policy owned on his or her life or other Florida resident is exempt from the claims of creditors, unless the policy was funded with the intent to defraud creditors.

Annuities

Perhaps the most popular financial product for asset protection planning is an annuity. Florida statutes protect annuities from creditors' claims and Florida courts have liberally construed this statutory exemption to include the broadest range of annuity contracts and arrangements. In fact, Florida protects not only annuities but also annuity payments received by a debtor, so long as they are accurately traceable back to the annuity. Private annuities between family members are entitled to the exemption as are the proceeds of personal injury settlements structured as an annuity.

Salary or Wages

Florida Statute § 222.11 exempts from creditors an unlimited amount of salary earned from personal labor or services by a debtor who is the head of household, if the debtor provides more than fifty percent of the support for a dependent (e.g., a child, spouse or parent). The statute defines "head of household" as "any natural person who is providing more than one half of the support for a child or other dependent." The wages remain exempt for a period of six months when deposited in a bank account.

Hurricane Saving Accounts

A recent addition to Florida's list of assets protected from creditors is the hurricane savings account. This account is protected under Florida Statute § 222.22 4(b). The statute defines a hurricane savings account as an account owned by the owner of homestead property up to twice the amount of an insurance deductible or other uninsurable portion of the risk of loss from a hurricane, windstorm or flood.

College 529 Savings Plans

Named for the section of the Internal Revenue Code that creates and regulates them, 529 plans provide a way for a parent or grandparent to invest and save for a descendant's education. Protection of these plans under Florida law depends on where the money is placed. If you invest in a 529 plan located in Florida, the fund is protected under Florida Statute § 222.22 pertaining to prepaid college trust funds.

Disability Income Benefits

Disability income benefits under any disability insurance policy are exempt from legal process in Florida.

Automobile Exemption

Florida residents may protect up to $1,000 of equity in an automobile. The fact that a debtor needs an automobile to go to work does not protect the vehicle from creditors to the extent that the debtor's equity (value less any loan amount) exceeds $1,000.

Miscellaneous Exemptions

Florida statutes include several other narrow asset exemptions, such as professionally prescribed health aids, medical saving accounts and unemployment benefits.

FLORIDA'S STATE PIE

The preferred pie of Floridians is the key lime pie. As the official state pie, it beat out its competitors: the pecan pie and sweet potato pie.

Key lime pies may have originated with the advent of condensed milk. Without many cows to give milk and no refrigeration, canned milk was popular when it was introduced in the 1850s and locals used it, along with the limes Spanish explorers had brought with them, to make the famous pie.

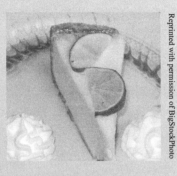

Reprinted with permission of BigStockPhoto

KEY LIME PIE RECIPE

4 large egg yolks

1 (14 oz.) can sweetened condensed milk

1/2 cup key lime juice

Baked 9 inch graham cracker crust

Whipped cream for garnish

*Beat eggs until thick and light yellow. Add sweetened condensed milk. Stir in half of the juice until blended. Add remaining juice and blend in. Pour mixture into pie shell. Bake at 350 degrees for 12 to 15 minutes until set. Cool pie and chill in refrigerator. Top with whipped cream before serving.

Graham Cracker Crust

Mix together:

1 1/4 cup graham cracker crumbs

1/4 cup sugar

1/3 cup butter or margarine, melted

*Press into bottom and up sides of a 9 inch pie pan. Bake in 375 degree oven for 6 to 8 minutes until lightly browned. Place on rack to cool.

Note: It can take up to 12 whole small key limes (6 Persian limes) to make 1/2 cup of the juice. You can use Persian limes, but I would substitute lemon juice for half the amount of juice to get the key lime flavor kick.

Hint: Peak key lime season is during the summer months. You can juice the limes and freeze them in ice cube trays then transfer them to sealable plastic bags where they can be stored in your freezer for future pie use.

Source: from the kitchen of Florida Domicile Handbook editor Mollie Page.

*Florida was to Americans what America had always been
to the rest of the world – a fresh, free, unspoiled start.*
The Orchid Thief
– Susan Orlean

CHAPTER 5

PART 1: QUESTIONS AND ANSWERS
BENEFITS OF FLORIDA DOMICILE

Homestead Exemption

Q: How do I file for the Florida homestead exemption?

A: Complete an application form (see sample in Appendix B2) in person at the office of the property appraiser. Clerks are always present to assist in filling out the form. Some county property appraisers allow you to mail in applications. Review the information in Chapter 3 to prepare yourself beforehand.

Q: Where can I file?

A: You can file at the property appraiser's main office weekdays from 8 a.m. to 5 p.m. In addition, many offices have sign-up tables in various locations (i.e., local malls) during January and February.

Q: What information do I need to bring with me?

A: You typically will need to bring the following:
- A recorded deed or tax bill in your name,
- Florida driver license,
- Florida auto tag registration,
- Voter registration card if you are a registered voter,

- Social Security numbers of all owners listed on the property and
- A declaration of domicile filed with the Clerk of the Circuit Court, if you have recorded one.

All documentation must be dated prior to January 1 of the tax year for which you are applying for the exemption. Please call the property appraiser's office to confirm the information you will need to supply. If the property is jointly owned, the property appraiser's office must have residency information on all owners residing on the property. You must have legal or equitable title to the property and reside there as a legal resident of Florida on or before January 1.

Q: Do I have to live in Florida for a period of time to file for the Florida homestead exemption?

A: No, there is no time limit for establishing Florida residency. What is important is your intention to make Florida your home. However, if you claim a Florida homestead but fail to spend a significant period of time within the state, your claim to exemption may be challenged by the property appraiser's office.

Q: When is the deadline for applying?

A: All exemption applications must be filed by March 1 if you are to receive the homestead exemption on January 1 of that year (affecting the assessment for the following year). Most Florida property appraiser's offices accept pre-filed applications throughout the year—to qualify for the following year.

Q: Do I have to be a U.S. citizen to qualify?

A: U.S. citizenship is not required to file for a homestead exemption. An applicant who is not a U.S. citizen must present a resident alien card (green card) when applying.

Q: What must I do if the home is in trust?

A: In such cases, it is necessary for the applicant to present a copy of the trust, so that eligibility of the trust to qualify for homestead exemption can be determined. The Florida Constitution requires that the homestead claimant have legal title or beneficial title in equity to the property.

Q: Is my homestead exemption transferable?

A: On January 29, 2008, Florida voters approved a change to the Florida Constitution that allows for the portability of the accumulated Save Our Homes benefit (limitation on the assessed valuation increases from year to year) up to a limit of $500,000 of exemption. When transferring to a home of lower value, a percentage (determined by dividing the value of the new home by the value of the prior home) is applied to the SOH benefit to be transferred.

Q: Can I get homestead exemption on a mobile home?

A: Yes, if your mobile home is permanently affixed to land that you own. When applying, you must bring in a recorded deed or copy of the tax bill to the real estate in your name as evidence of ownership and the title or registration to the mobile home.

Q: Is there any appeal if I miss the deadline?

A: Yes. You may file a late application for homestead exemption in person at the property appraiser's office until the last day (call the appraiser's office to find out the exact date) to file a petition with the Value Adjustment Board (VAB). The VAB panel or a special master will hear your reasons for not filing in a timely manner and make a determination whether or not your application can be approved for that tax year.

Q: Are there any other benefits to having a homestead exemption?

A: Yes. The homestead exemption has taken on additional

importance since the passage of Amendment X to the Florida Constitution, "Save Our Homes," which caps assessments. Eligibility applies only to homesteaded properties. The amendment states that the assessed value increase cannot exceed the lesser of 3 percent or the increase in the consumer price index (CPI), each year following the year you received your homestead exemption. Also, there is an additional homestead exemption of up to $25,000 for certain persons age 65 years or older. To qualify for the additional exemption, the household income (i.e., cumulative adjusted gross income) of all persons living in the home cannot exceed a yearly amount as determined by the Florida Department of Revenue. To obtain the extra exemption, your application must be made annually.

Q: What other exemptions are available under law?

A: State law entitles you to apply for an additional exemption as a widow or widower. Some medical disabilities may also qualify for an additional exemption. To inquire about other exemptions to which you may be entitled, contact the county property appraiser in the county where you reside.

Q: If I am married and the homestead is in my name alone, will I be able to transfer the residence as I desire?

A: Attempts at transferring the homestead residence can have severe repercussions if not done properly. Any transfer during your life may result in a loss of creditor protection, a loss of the Save Our Homes component of the homestead exemption, or violate rules with respect to restrictions on transfer. If you are planning on making a transfer of your homestead property, you should seek advice from an attorney who is competent in dealing with all aspects of homestead.

QUESTIONS AND ANSWERS

Estate Planning

Q: What is estate planning?

A: Proper estate planning is "living planning," providing for you and your family during life and preparing for the orderly and efficient transfer of your assets at your death. The process of good estate planning involves the preparation of various documents, such as wills, trusts and powers of attorney.

Virtually every plan should start with the goal of allowing you to give what you have to whom you want when you want and in the way you want and, at the same time, paying the least amount of court costs, attorney's fees and estate taxes possible. The process often includes life insurance planning and the use of irrevocable life insurance trusts, revocable living trusts and other ancillary documents, such as living wills and health care powers of attorney.

The "living" part of estate planning includes taking care of your family in the event you become incapacitated during your lifetime; charitable giving strategies that can provide for you and other family members during your life and one or more charities at your death; and retirement planning, gift and income tax planning and protection from creditors.

Q: Does federal or state law govern estate taxes?

A: On the federal level, estate and gift taxes, income tax and generation-skipping transfer tax are governed by the Internal Revenue Code and its regulations and rules. The federal courts settle disputes between taxpayers and the IRS regarding these rules.

Each state, including Florida, has its own statutes with regard to inheritance and gift taxes, as well as wills, trusts, partnerships and so on. Florida courts interpret state statutes in case of disagreements.

Q: Does Florida have a state gift or inheritance tax?

A: No. Before the enactment of the Economic Growth and Tax Relief Reconciliation Act (EGTRRA) of 2001, Florida, like many states, relied on receiving a portion of the tax charged by the federal estate tax system. This tax was often referred to as a "sponge" or "pickup tax" and often was the only death-related tax charged by the states. However, EGTRRA ended the sharing program and many states have decoupled from the federal system. Thus, many states have enacted separate gift or estate taxes (aka "inheritance" tax, if paid by the beneficiary) for their residents.

Florida's Constitution mandates full conformity with the federal law under EGTRRA and does not allow the imposition of a decoupled state estate or gift tax. Hence, until there is a change in its Constitution, Florida does not have a state gift or estate tax.

Q: Why should I do my estate planning in Florida?

A: Here are some of the many reasons to do your estate planning in Florida:

- Florida has no separate state estate, inheritance or gift tax.
- Florida laws allow you to establish a trust that will last up to 360 years—protecting the assets in trust for your heirs for several generations.
- Florida has no income tax, so the earnings on trust assets in your Florida trust(s) will not be subject to state income tax.
- Florida no longer has an intangibles tax.

If any part of your estate is exposed to probate, the probate process in Florida is relatively simple and can be done in a timely fashion.

A significant number of Florida-based attorneys, CPAs, trust officers, financial planners and insurance professionals specialize in family wealth transfer planning.

Q. I have recently done my estate planning in my previous state. Why should I redo my planning in Florida?

A. Estate and probate laws vary from state to state. Consequently, if you are relocating to Florida, you should review the peculiarities of Florida law with a qualified Florida estate planning attorney to determine the appropriateness and effectiveness of your current estate plan. Although you may not need to rewrite your entire estate plan, there may be good reasons for considering some revisions or additions. In addition, to help establish intent, your estate planning documents should reflect that you are now a Florida resident.

Q: Is my out-of-state will effective in Florida?

A: Most states, including Florida, recognize an out-of-state will as valid as long as it is written and executed according to the requirements of the state in which it was signed. To help establish intent, your will should be revised to show that you are a Florida resident.

Q: If I relocate my domicile to Florida, will I owe any tax in my former state of residence at my death?

A: Your estate may be subject to death taxation in another state if you own real property or certain other tangible assets in that state or if that state successfully claims that you are domiciled there at the time of your death. Depending on the laws of that state and the type of estate tax imposed, there are additional steps that you may take as a Florida resident to minimize the impact of any such tax.

Q: Now that I am becoming a Florida resident, should I change my personal representative and trustee in my out-of-state planning documents?

A: If your will names a nonresident individual as personal representative, he or she will not be allowed to qualify in Florida unless related to you in the manner provided by Florida statute.

If your will names an out-of-state trust company or bank as your personal representative or trustee, you should confirm that the trust company or bank will be qualified to exercise fiduciary powers in Florida. If you have a trust that names an individual residing far from Florida as trustee, it may not be practical to expect such an individual to carry out his or her responsibilities.

Q: Are provisions of my will subject to different legal interpretations under Florida Law?

A: Laws governing the interpretation of wills vary from state to state. Your will should be reviewed by a Florida attorney to determine whether Florida law may defeat your estate planning goals. For example, you may have a provision attempting to pass your Florida homestead property to someone in violation of Florida law; the provision would be unenforceable in Florida.

Q: What effect does Florida law have on me if my spouse and I have moved to Florida from a community property state?

A. Community property affects the rights of you and your spouse in determining certain income and estate tax liabilities, as well as property rights under Florida law. If you are relocating to Florida from a community property state, you should meet with an estate planning professional to review your estate plan to avoid unanticipated and undesirable tax consequences. For example, community property is entitled to federal income tax benefits that can be preserved even if you become domiciled in Florida.

Q: After relocating to Florida, when do estate planning documents need to be reviewed?

A: Virtually all estate plans should be reviewed when there has been one or more changes in your life, such as a birth, death, remarriage, a change in your financial picture or move to another state (i.e., Florida). You should also consider meeting with your Florida attorney or financial planner when there has been a change in the tax laws. Beyond that, it makes good sense to review your estate plan documents with your advisers every two or three years to be sure they still meet your estate planning goals and to take advantage of any new planning strategies.

Q: What is the biggest problem in estate planning?

A: The biggest problem in estate planning is procrastination. It is human nature to put off things that seem distasteful, but ignoring estate planning may hurt those you love most. And with proper planning, you can realize many living benefits.

Over 70 percent of those who died last year in the United States did so without a will or any planning whatsoever. Many of those people would turn over in their graves if they could discover what happened to the assets they left behind.

If you die without an estate plan, you die intestate, allowing the state to dictate how your assets will pass among your heirs. The state's plan often does not come close to matching what you would really want to happen. In Florida, if you are married, only half of your assets will pass to your spouse if you have children; the other half will pass to your children, immediately and outright. This distribution could have a dramatic and undesirable effect on the family. When it comes to estate planning, the old adage "it is better to show a dead horse than a live one" does not apply.

Q: Should my children be brought into the estate planning process?

A: While it may feel uncomfortable to discuss estate planning matters with children, it often makes good sense to do so. Giving adult children a summary view of your estate plan can avoid unnecessary problems or misunderstandings that can occur after you are dead.

When people die, it is not unusual for family members to get into disputes because a parent's intentions were never clarified. Even if you don't discuss specific amounts with your children, you should consider discussing the structure of your estate plan.

Q: What is the role of the probate court?

A: A probate court is the forum in which legal proceedings occur if you are no longer able to manage your affairs because of your incapacity, mental disability or your death.

THE FAMOUS FLORIDA KEYS

The Florida Keys run south for approximately 100 miles from Key Largo to Key West and include uninhabited islands. Major cities in the Florida Keys include Key Largo, Islamorada, Marathon and Key West. Key West is famous for its bars, nightlife, art and history. Visitors enjoy touring Ernest Hemingway's house and gathering in Mallory Square to watch the sun set. Fishing, snorkeling and scuba diving are available throughout the Keys. A concession at Bahia Honda State Park takes guests to Looe Key, one of the best snorkeling sites. For the adventurous, day trips depart from Key West to the Dry Tortugas, 60 miles away. There are even places near Key West where you can arrange to swim with dolphins.

Reprinted with permission of BigStockPhoto

In the case of death, the probate court process transfers ownership of assets titled in your individual name to your heirs. In effect, probate is the process of proving the validity of your will. This process can take weeks, months or even years to complete, depending upon the size, complexity and design of your estate plan. With proper planning (i.e., through the use of a fully funded revocable living trust), it is possible to completely avoid, where desirable, the probate process and the court administration that follows the proving of the will.

The probate process in Florida is relatively simple and is often completed in a reasonable period of time; however, there are other aspects to consider, such as the cost of probate and the public nature of probate proceedings.

In the event you are incapacitated, you and your family must contend with the guardianship process, which is, in essence, a living probate. Guardianship is designed to protect you and your assets while you are incapable of doing so yourself. Guardianship can be an expensive and time-consuming process.

Like the probate process, guardianship can often be avoided completely with a properly funded revocable living trust.

Q: I have a will. Doesn't that mean my heirs will avoid probate?

A: No. It is a mistake to assume that by having a will you have eliminated probate. Just the opposite is true; unless your assets are titled in a manner that avoids probate, a will very nearly guarantees probate because only a court can prove the validity of a will.

Q: What is so bad about probate?

A: There are numerous reasons why it is best to avoid probate, even in Florida where the probate process is considered to be less complex than in many other states. Some of those reasons include:

Cost: In many states the cost associated with probating your estate, including attorney fees, probate costs, appraisals and so on, generally ranges from 3 to 15 percent of the value of the estate. In Florida your family may experience real savings in legal fees if you incorporate a properly funded RLT into your estate plan.

Time delay: Probate takes time and in many states, including Florida, probate can easily take a year or more before the estate is fully settled. Depending upon the size of your estate or the nature of your assets, you can save your family excessive time delays if you minimize or eliminate your exposure to probate.

Complexity: If you have property, such as real estate, in more than one state, your heirs will likely face separate probate proceedings in each state where the property is located. These multiple probates, called ancillary administration, can significantly add to the cost and time delay of settling an estate.

Public exposure: Although your financial information may not be available to the public, the terms of your will may very well be open to public inspection.

Contests: The public nature of the court process may make it easier for unwanted third parties such as disgruntled family members, ex-spouses, in-laws and creditors to contest the estate.

Q: What is the best way to avoid probate?

A: Assets held in an RLT are not subject to the probate process. Although there are limitations to any trust arrangement, if your objective is to avoid the cost, time delays, publicity and complexity inherent in the probate process, an RLT is often the best method to accomplish this. Certain assets, such as a bank account or brokerage account, may pass by designation (called a transfer or pay-on-death designation). Although such a designation may avoid a probate, the asset with such a designation could still get caught up in the guardianship process if you become incompetent.

Q: Why not simply put everything in joint tenancy to avoid probate?

A: Joint tenancy with the right of survivorship (or tenancy by the entirety between spouses) is one of the most common and simplest forms of estate planning. When the first of the joint tenants dies, the jointly owned assets pass, by law, to the other "tenant," completely avoiding probate. If the remaining joint tenant is a spouse, no estate tax would normally be due. However, there are hidden risks associated with this planning strategy.

Each joint tenant can be held responsible for actions of the other tenant. For example, titling an automobile jointly with a spouse or child who later becomes involved in an accident can cause you to be named as a defendant in a lawsuit resulting from that accident.

You could lose control of bank accounts, stock accounts, annuities, mutual funds and so forth, because either joint tenant may be able to sell such assets without the permission or knowledge of the other owner.

If one joint owner has a problem with a creditor or judgment in a lawsuit, the other owner could lose the asset through court action or garnishment. Although this problem may be avoided with a special form of joint tenancy between spouses, known as "tenancy by the entirety," protection could be lost if one spouse dies. For example, assume a married couple owns an asset as tenants by the entirety and the husband has a judgment against him (but not his wife). In this case, the asset is protected from the husband's creditor. However, if the wife predeceases the husband, the protection is lost.

Some jointly held property cannot be sold if one of the joint owners either cannot, because of illness, or will not sign.

Joint tenancy can also result in unintended disinheritance. For example, Jason and Amy both have a child and grandchildren from previous marriages. If Jason dies first and their property is held jointly, Amy can disinherit Jason's child and grandchildren by leaving the asset to her child and grandchildren.

There may be gift tax implications. For example, Louise purchased a Florida condominium and titled it in her name and her stepdaughter's name as joint owner. By doing so, Louise may have made a gift to her stepdaughter equal to 50 percent of the value of the home. Louise exposed herself to a substantial federal gift tax on the amounts above any unused exemption she elects to use towards the gift.

Beneficiaries receive the assets all at once, even when they may not be able to manage them. Also, a spouse who dies first may not be able to use his or her exemption when their assets are held jointly, potentially exposing part of their estate to estate taxes unnecessarily.

If the joint tenants die in a common accident, each tenant, depending upon state law, is entitled to one-half of the assets, which would then cause two probate proceedings.

Q: Is probate ever desirable?

A. Florida probate laws are designed to settle creditor's claims quickly upon a decedent's death (e.g., possibly as short as three months, although a year is common). In the absence of a probate proceeding, creditors claims may not be completely settled for two years after a decedent's death.

Q: What is the purpose of a will?

A: A will allows you to direct who will receive your assets at the time of your death. Without a will or a will substitute (e.g., RLT), you will die intestate. As a Florida resident, Florida will determine the distribution of your assets in accordance with Florida's intestacy laws.

Your will is revocable during your lifetime. It does not avoid probate. It directs the probate court regarding your wishes. Your will does not control property that you hold as a joint tenant. Also, life insurance, annuities, IRAs and qualified plan assets pass to your heirs—by a separate document known as a beneficiary designation—outside of the will unless you have named your estate as your beneficiary in that document.

Wills can create trusts at your death, known as testamentary trusts, or a will can direct that specific assets be distributed ("poured over") to a preexisting trust at your death. Wills cannot, however, provide for your care in the event you become incapacitated or disabled.

Q: What is a revocable living trust?

A: A revocable living trust (RLT) is a legal document typically drafted by an attorney. It acts like a will in that it contains your directions for the management and distribution of your assets upon your death. Unlike a will, however, an RLT also contains your instructions for the management of your assets in the event of your disability.

You are the grantor (or trust maker) of the trust agreement and you and possibly your spouse, if named, are beneficiaries of the trust during your lifetime. In most situations you would name yourself and possibly your spouse as trustees. Thus, you continue to control and manage your assets like you did before you set up the RLT.

To avoid probate, you need to fund your trust by transferring or retitling your assets from your name to yourself (or whomever else you designate) as trustee of your trust. As trustee of your own RLT, you maintain full control over trust property during your lifetime. You also continue to file your income tax returns as you have in the past (using your social security number) and can buy, sell or give away trust property. With this control, you can change, alter or revoke the terms of the trust any time you wish.

At your death, the trust may terminate or, depending upon your instructions, continue for the benefit of your family and other heirs. Much like a will, your RLT contains instructions on how you want the trust assets distributed (e.g., outright or continue in trust) to your beneficiaries at your death. A Florida trust can be designed to split into two or more trusts (e.g., one for each beneficiary) and continue for up to 360 years.

Q: How does an RLT avoid probate?

A: When an RLT is properly funded with all your assets, there is no need to probate the trust assets as the RLT is still "alive." This is true whether you are incapacitated or dead. The RLT merely continues on in accordance with the terms of your trust.

Q: Why do I need an RLT if I become disabled?

A: Without an RLT that provides for your care during any disability, your loved ones may have to take you through the legal process of a "living" probate, or guardianship, with the help of attorneys and a probate judge. Even though your spouse or adult children would most likely be appointed by the court to manage your affairs, they would have to report annually to the court and would be subject to all the legal costs and red tape of the court system. This cumbersome and often needlessly bureaucratic court process would likely continue for as long as you are disabled.

FLORIDA'S BIG TOP PIONEER

Along with four of his six brothers, John Ringling created the Ringling Brothers Circus and helped define the traveling circus. In 1927, the brothers moved the circus's winter headquarters to Sarasota on Florida's west coast. The Ringling legacy lives on at the John and Mable Ringling Museum of Art in Sarasota. It hosts a museum dedicated to the circus, twenty-one art galleries and the Ringling's restored oceanfront mansion, the Cà d'Zan.

An RLT allows you to choose, in detail, how you want your affairs handled and permits you to set the priorities that you want followed. Furthermore, your successor trustees will be able to manage your financial and other affairs beginning the moment you are incapacitated without the intervention and potential delays of any court.

Q. Do I need an RLT if I have a durable power of attorney?

A. Yes. Even though a durable power of attorney is designed to be effective if you become incapacitated, the power of attorney may be of no use if a court declares you to be incompetent and imposes a guardianship (despite your attempt to avoid guardianship) or a financial institution declines to honor the document.

Generally speaking, it is not a good idea to leave anything of any consequence to your loved ones outright or "free of trust." By leaving everything in trust for your heirs' benefit, you can protect them in ways they cannot achieve for themselves.

For example, you could specify in your trust that each of your children is to serve as the trustee of his or her own separate trust, alone or along with one or more co-trustees for his or her lifetime, and that each child's trust provide for their needs as they arise. It would allow each child to manage his or her own funds in the way he or she desires; yet, by retaining everything in trust, you have to some degree protected each child's assets from the claims of creditors, which could arise from a failed business venture, an accident or even a spouse in a divorce.

By leaving assets in trust, you may be concerned that your children will think you are controlling them from the grave. However, with the assistance of a qualified attorney, you may be able to provide a great deal of latitude to your children without jeopardizing the benefits of a trust. A qualified attorney can draft your trust in accordance with your wishes, with terms that are as restrictive or liberal as you choose.

Q: Do I need a will if I have an RLT?

A: Yes. A revocable living trust is very powerful and, effectively, acts as your will. However, because many people fail to transfer all their assets into (or "fully fund") their RLT, you should also execute a pour-over will, which acts as a safety net and instructs your executor or personal representative to place those assets in your RLT, after going through probate, so that they can be managed and distributed according to the instructions in your trust.

To avoid subjecting any portion of your estate to probate, you should periodically review how your assets are titled to make sure all appropriate assets are titled in your name, as trustee of your trust. Note that some assets should not be titled in your RLT, such as annuities and retirement plan assets.

Annuities and retirement plan assets, including IRAs, can pass at your death by a beneficiary designation form if you complete one before your death. Another asset that you should seriously consider leaving outside your RLT is your Florida homestead.

Your Florida homestead, aside from being one of your most valuable assets, is given a great deal of protection from creditors. However, a question arose a few years ago in federal bankruptcy court whether a Florida homestead loses its creditor protection if it is owned in an RLT. Although Florida law is quite clear that the Florida homestead would still be protected if owned by an RLT, the uncertainty caused by the federal bankruptcy court suggests that you should own your home outside an RLT.

Q: If I have an RLT, will it help my family avoid paying estate taxes?

A: A properly funded RLT avoids probate at your death. However, probate and the federal estate tax have nothing to do with each other. To save federal estate taxes, your attorney could incorporate certain estate tax planning provisions into your RLT.

One such strategy for spouses who plan to leave everything to each other on the first death is to make sure that your revocable living trust directs the portion of your estate equaling the remainder of your estate tax exemption to a credit shelter (bypass, family or "B") trust to avoid wasting your exemption. Your spouse could be the trustee and a named beneficiary of the B trust. Thus, he or she would have access, as needed, but the assets would not be included in his or her taxable estate.

Q: Does an RLT protect me from creditors?

A: No. As trustee of your RLT, you have the ability to control the assets in your trust and, as the trust maker, you have the ability to revoke the trust at any time. Thus, the assets in an RLT are at the same risk in the event of a judgment against you as they would be if they were titled directly in your name. However, it is possible to design your trust to protect your assets from your beneficiaries' creditors—including spouses in a divorce situation—after your death.

Q: Who should be my trustee after I die or become disabled?

A: You can name more than one trustee, but whomever you select should be someone you trust. Your successor trustee should be a person (or persons) or institution that you have confidence in and that has the ability to handle financial matters. In addition, the trustee you select should be familiar with your objectives and should carry out distributions according to the guidelines you have established in your RLT and overall estate plan.

You should also make sure that the person or institution will accept the responsibilities of being your trustee. Furthermore, it is always wise to name alternate trustees in case your initial choices should later be unable or unwilling to serve as trustee.

Q: What is so important about funding an RLT?

A: One of the biggest mistakes in estate planning is failing to "fund" or transfer ownership of your assets to yourself, as trustee of your RLT. By failing to fund your RLT, you have guaranteed that those assets not titled in the trust will end up going through probate—which is the very thing you were trying to avoid and one of the primary reasons for setting up the trust.

Q: How do I fund my RLT?

A: Funding your trust is not difficult and your financial advisers can likely help you. For example, your estate planning attorney can help prepare the appropriate deeds to transfer real estate and your financial adviser, CPA or stockbroker can help you transfer other financial assets, such as investment and bank accounts, to your RLT.

GEOGRAPHY: SOUTH FLORIDA

South Florida refers primarily to Florida's southeast coast, from Ft. Pierce south to Key West. The major cities in South Florida are Miami, Fort Lauderdale and West Palm Beach. Visitors flock to Miami Beach for its Latin vibe and wild nightlife. Miami is also home to the Miami Dolphins, the Marlins, the Miami Heat, Miami Seaquarium, Fairchild Tropical Gardens and countless shopping opportunities. Motorboat and jet ski rental concessions are plentiful. Just north, Palm Beach County offers some of the best golfing in Florida and Everglades National Park is a short drive west, with wildlife viewing, airboat tours, canoeing and camping.

FACTS ABOUT SOUTH FLORIDA

Miami Beach pharmacist Benjamin Green invented the first suntan cream in 1944. He accomplished this development by cooking cocoa butter in a granite coffee pot on his wife's stove.

Key West has the highest average temperature in the United States—at just above 78 degrees Fahrenheit.

Miami installed the first automated bank teller machine especially for inline skaters.

The Morikami Museum and Japanese Gardens, on 200 acres at Delray Beach, is the only museum in the United States dedicated exclusively to the living culture of Japan.

Fort Lauderdale is known as the Venice of America because the city has 185 miles of local waterways.

Islamorada is billed as Sports Fishing Capital of the World.

Key Largo is known as the Diving Capital of the World.

Fort Zachary Taylor in Key West was built between 1845 and 1866. Controlled by the Union during the Civil War, the fort was the home base for a successful blockade of Confederate ships that some historians say shortened the conflict by a full year. The fort also was active during the Spanish-American War, World War I and World War II.

The Florida Museum of Hispanic and Latin American Art in Coral Gables is the first and only museum in the United States dedicated to the preservation, diffusion and promotion of Hispanic and Latin American Art.

Source: www.50states.com/facts/florida.htm.

Q: When I retitle my assets, will I need to give a copy of my RLT to the various financial institutions?

A: Yes. To protect themselves from potential legal liability, your investment brokerage firm and bank will need to know who has authority to act on your behalf. Thus, it is likely they will ask for a copy of the trust. However, it is usually sufficient to supply them with a portion of your RLT, such as the cover page, signature page and the section listing your authority, as trustee, over the trust assets. Alternatively, many estate planning attorneys provide a short document—sometimes known as a memorandum of trust or affidavit of trust—that will often suffice.

Q: Since my RLT acts as my will, what type of information should be included in the trust?

A: Just as in the preparation of your will, you should consider the following questions:

- Who do you want to inherit your assets and in what amounts or percentages?
- What should be the timing of the distributions of your assets to your various heirs?
- Who would you like to receive specific assets, such as your personal effects (e.g., car, watch, jewelry and artwork)?
- Should you leave assets outright or, as suggested above, in one or more trusts?
- If you decide on leaving assets in trust, who should be the trustee of each trust?
- Does it make sense to have a co-trustee, such as a trust company, for certain trusts for a period of time or for the life of the trust?

Q: Am I required by Florida law to leave a certain portion of my estate to my surviving spouse?

A: Under the laws of Florida, your surviving spouse may "elect" to receive 30 percent of your estate (plus the value of certain lifetime transfers) at your death even if such a gift would be against your wishes. This right is called the elective share. You should consult with an attorney to ensure that your estate plan properly takes the elective share into account.

For example, your estate plan may be designed to hold your spouse's elective share in trust (rather than being distributed outright to your spouse). Note that a spouse's right to an elective share at your death may be restricted or eliminated with a pre- or postmarital agreement.

Q: Is it possible to distribute a portion of my estate to my children and other heirs upon my death and the remainder of my assets to them upon my spouse's death?

A: Yes. However, it is important to consider the tax ramifications of making distributions to anyone other than your spouse. There is an unlimited marital deduction on gifts to your spouse during your lifetime and at your death. If distributions to your heirs, other than your spouse, do not exceed your remaining applicable federal estate exemption at your death, no federal estate tax would be due. However, if you are not domiciled in Florida, your state of residence may have a state inheritance tax and an exemption below the current federal estate tax exemption, thereby exposing your estate to state taxes. If you are domiciled in Florida and own real estate in another state with an estate tax, your estate may have to pay tax if the value of the real estate is above that state's specific exemption.

Note that you should always consult an estate planning attorney when designing your estate plan. This is especially true if your spouse is not a U.S. citizen.

Tax issues aside, you are generally free to distribute your property at death any way you wish, subject to your surviving spouse's rights, as discussed above, and claims by your creditors.

Q: What will happen if I become incapacitated?

A: Many people fail to address the question of incapacity (incompetency) before it becomes a serious issue. By not acting, you may be unnecessarily subjecting your family to the probate court and all its administrative bureaucracy. Failing to provide for someone to look after you in the event of your incapacity will cause the court to appoint a guardian for you. These individuals or institutions may or may not be the persons or organizations you would choose if you were able to do so. And even if they are, you would likely incur the expenses and delays of the judicial process.

To avoid what could be a bureaucratic nightmare, your RLT should appoint one or more successor trustees who will "take over" for you during your period of disability. In addition, in a separate document known as a special durable power of attorney for funding, you should authorize one or more individuals to transfer property that is not in your RLT specifically to your RLT so that your trustee can use it to care for you during your disability under the terms of your trust.

Q: How do I arrange for someone to be able to make health care decisions for me in the event I am unable to do so?

A: Florida law allows you to designate a health care surrogate to make health care decisions, including whether to remove life support, in the event you are unable to make such decisions yourself.

Q: Should I provide for how I want my personal property distributed?

A: Yes. You can make up a written instrument, often referred to as a memorandum of tangible personal property, to control the manner in which you want your personal effects distributed. This document should be kept with your RLT.

Q: I am considering retiring in Florida, but want to be certain my dog is cared for when I am gone. Does Florida allow pets to "inherit"?

A: Yes, Florida is a pet-friendly state and allows the creation of a trust to provide for the care and well-being of an animal. Speak to your Florida attorney about including a clause to benefit your dog and other pets in your estate planning papers.

THE NEXT GENERATION IN SPACE

The Constellation Program, NASA's human space flight program, was excluded from President Barack Obama's federal budget for 2011. This leaves a black hole in the hearts of many Americans that envisioned human space exploration into the future.

The three "soon-to-be-retired" shuttles – The Discovery, The Endeavor and The Atlantis – will be placed in museums across the country, with Discovery heading to the Smithsonian Air and Space Museum in Washington D.C. Since the first flight in 1981, the space shuttle fleet has completed more than 100 missions and carried more than 600 passengers into space. The fleet has accumulated more than 2.5 years in orbit and yet has 75 percent of its design life remaining.

But the Kennedy Space Center is not closing! In fact, the Center is redirecting some of the Constellation program money into building a Center of Excellence (COE) for Commercial Space Transportation. This new initiative partners with universities and will perform research and development to help build a safe and strong U.S. commercial space industry. The Kennedy Center will also serve as a flight test center for COE research efforts.

Space Fact: On May 5, 2011, the 50th anniversary of the first U.S. manned spaceflight will be celebrated. This commemorates Alan Shepard's Mercury Freedom 7 suborbital flight on May 5, 1961.

Source: NASA

"I'd like you to meet my children, Occupant
and Resident."

PART 2

HOW TO ESTABLISH FLORIDA DOMICILE

Your "domicile" and your "residence" are not necessarily the same. You may have more than one residence in more than one state but, for tax purposes, you have only one domicile. Your domicile is a subjective concept and principally a matter of intent; it is where you intend your home base to be; it is your true, fixed and permanent state of residence. However, if you do not properly establish a clear domicile, it is possible that your "former" state of domicile may claim you as a "resident" of that state and tax you accordingly.

Where you are domiciled at your death can have a significant impact on the taxation of your estate. While nearly all states claim that a person can have only one domicile, each state has the right to apply its own definition of domicile. To complicate matters, federal tax law does not alleviate the problem with a definition of its own.

For example, when Howard Hughes died, multiple states wanted to tax his estate. The U.S. Supreme Court refused to settle the dispute, ruling that each state had the authority to impose its estate tax on domiciled residents.

In another famous case, the states of Florida, Texas, New York and Massachusetts each claimed Colonel Edward H. R. Green, son of the legendary Hetty Green, was domiciled in their state at the time of his death and entitled to collect death taxes on his tangible property within the state and on his intangible property wherever located. None of the states had reduced its tax claim to a judgment, but all conceded that the decedent's estate was insufficient to satisfy the total amount of taxes claimed.

Similarly, in the case of Hill vs. Martin, the U. S. Supreme Court allowed Pennsylvania and New Jersey both to claim domicile and tax the estate of Dr. John Thompson Dorrance, the founder of the Campbell Soup Company. As a result, each state collected approximately $17 million in state estate taxes from his estate.

It is important to note that, for purposes of estate tax, real or tangible property (i.e., real estate, automobiles, jewelry, etc.) may be subject to tax in the state where the property is located, regardless of your domicile. However, intangible property (i.e., stocks, bonds, notes, bank accounts, etc.) will generally be taxed only in the state of your domicile. Since Florida does not currently have an estate or gift tax, no state tax would be due on intangible assets or on tangible assets located in Florida that are gifted or bequeathed to others—from someone who has established Florida domicile. Thus, if you have real or personal property in multiple states, depending upon the location of those assets at the time of your death, there may be some tax due.

Clearly establishing Florida as your state of domicile can help you avoid unnecessary imposition of state estate or inheritance taxes in multiple states. Through careful planning, you can not only avoid exposure to multiple taxation, but you can potentially eliminate state estate taxes.

NOTES

ACTION STEPS TO PROVE YOUR INTENT

By failing to prepare you are preparing to fail.
– Ben Franklin

CHAPTER 6

CHANGING YOUR DOMICILE: A STEP-BY-STEP GUIDE

When you make the decision to establish a Florida domicile, you must support your intent with action. Listed on the next few pages are steps to show your intent to change your domicile to Florida. Although not all the steps discussed below are required, the more steps you take, the stronger your case that you have established Florida domicile and abandoned your former domicile. Think of it as an apothecary scale and try to tip the scale to one side–Florida Domicile–by **taking as many of the following steps as possible.**

- File a declaration of domicile with the Clerk of Courts in the Florida county where you now reside. See sample form in Appendix B1.

- Spend as much time in Florida as is practical (preferably more than 180 days per year) and own or lease and occupy a residence in Florida.

- Obtain a Florida driver license.

- Register and license your cars, boats and vehicles in Florida.

- Register to vote in Florida (be sure to notify the voting registrar in your former state to remove your name from its voting records).

- File your federal income tax returns in Atlanta, Georgia, and notify the taxing authorities in your former state of your change of domicile.

- Discontinue filing tax returns in the state where you were formerly domiciled, except if your income has its source in that state (e.g., rental income generated by real estate located in your former state), in which case "nonresident" returns should be filed. If applicable, mark your last state income tax return in the state of your former domicile as the "final tax return."

- Establish relationships with Florida attorneys, doctors, accountants, brokers, financial planners, trust officers and insurance agents.

- Transfer financial assets (e.g., securities, bank accounts and brokerage accounts) to institutions in Florida or Florida offices of financial institutions used in your former state.

- Maintain a safe deposit box in Florida rather than in your former state (based on at least one court case, this could be a small but crucial factor in determining your domicile).

- When registering at hotels, state you are a Florida resident.

- Transact business in Florida and declare Florida your state of domicile in all written communications concerning your principal residence. Use your Florida address on all legal documents like deeds, leases, contracts, securities, etc.

- Estate planning documents, such as wills, trusts, living wills, health care proxies and powers of attorney, should state that you are domiciled in Florida. Have existing documents reviewed by a Florida attorney to conform to Florida law.

- Where possible, withdraw your membership from non-Florida clubs or institutions where residence in your former state is a prerequisite to membership and establish affiliations with social and religious organizations in Florida.

- Request a change to "nonresident" status for organizations in your former state of domicile—if you plan to maintain those affiliations.

- Change your mailing address and use your Florida address for all correspondence.

- Change your address on all credit cards, charge accounts, corporations, partnerships and trusts to your Florida address.

- Transfer family possessions, paintings, heirlooms and collections to Florida.

- While it is not necessary to own a home, mobile home or condominium in Florida, the commitment to ownership would be further evidence of your intent. Also, if you change your Florida location frequently (e.g., because you travel around Florida in a motor home), you should establish a place to receive your mail, such as a private mailbox or post office box, in Florida.

- If you own a home in Florida, file for homestead exemption.

- Celebrate special family occasions in Florida.

Multiple Domiciles

The loss of tax revenue has prompted many state taxing authorities to assert income and estate tax claims against their former residents. As discussed previously, it is constitutionally permissible for more than one state to tax you and your estate on the basis of domicile. Consult your financial adviser and attorney on the best way to minimize your exposure to "double" domicile claims, particularly if you continue to own real estate in another state.

For example, it may be a good idea to form a family limited liability company or family limited partnership and transfer the real estate located in other states to that entity. It may help avoid unwanted domicile claims and may possibly limit your exposure to state estate or inheritance taxes on those assets (see Chapter 4, "Estate Planning for Florida Residents").

Students

A student seeking Florida residency classification must demonstrate that he or she has established a bona fide domicile in Florida rather than maintaining a temporary residence that is incidental to being enrolled in a Florida university. To establish domicile, a student would have to take many of the steps discussed previously, along with some special steps that require establishing and maintaining a legal Florida residence for at least 12 months prior to the first day of classes in the semester for which in-state residency status is sought (see Chapter 12 for more details).

Split Domicile

Some prospective Florida residents feel that splitting domicile between themselves and a spouse will allow them to have the best of all worlds. While there are circumstances that could call for splitting domicile, it may not be advisable. For one thing, Florida will not allow you to retain your Florida homestead exemption if your spouse is claiming a homestead exemption in another state.

Furthermore, a split domicile raises other important issues. For example, some states require a married couple to file a joint state income tax return if the couple files a joint federal income tax return. In addition, depending on your timing, a split domicile may limit the amount of your total federal capital gain exclusion (from $500,000 to $250,000) for the sale of a principal residence after one spouse changes domicile.

Before attempting a split domicile, be sure to consult with a Florida attorney and carefully consider the potential advantages and disadvantages.

THE EDISON EFFECT

Thomas Alva Edison
1847 - 1931

Though most famous for his invention of the light bulb, Thomas Edison was also the inventor of many ground-breaking technologies, including the phonograph and the stock ticker. In 1885, at the age of 38, he purchased a winter residence in what was then the small town of Fort Myers. Here, he constructed the laboratory that was to be the site of some of his most important experiments.

Visited often by fellow entrepreneurs, Henry Ford and Harvey Firestone, Edison was encouraged by his friends to discover a source of natural rubber from native plants. In 1927, the three entrepreneurs founded the Edison Botanic Research Corporation with its lab situated in his Fort Myers home.

In 1947, the Edison Estate opened to the public. In 1990, the City of Fort Myers purchased the Ford home, located next door to the Edison estate. Visit the official Web site at www.efwefla.org.

Declaration of Domicile

Assuming you are not going to split your domicile between you and your spouse, both you and your spouse will have to declare Florida domicile on separate declaration of domicile forms. Some counties will allow a married couple to use one form. A sample is included in Appendix B1.

When you prepare to establish your domicile in Florida, you will probably wonder which steps to take first. The five steps below will help save you unnecessary work and make the process easier.

1. Fill out and file your declaration of domicile form(s) and either mail or deliver the form(s) to the court house in the county in which you reside. You can obtain the form from your financial advisor, attorney or the clerk of courts in the county you wish. Not all counties will accept mailed forms. Also, it may be possible to drop off the declaration at your local office of the Florida Driver License Bureau. Both you and your spouse should file a declaration. There is a small fee for recording each one-page document.

2. Obtain your Florida driver license at any office of the Florida Driver License Bureau. In addition to your present driver license from your former state, you may be required to show a copy of your birth certificate or passport.

3. Register to vote. This can be done at most Florida Driver License Bureau offices (through the "Motor-Voter" Program). You may also be able to register at your public library. Otherwise, you can register in your county's Supervisor of Elections Office. You can find more information on voting in Florida in Chapters 8 and 9.

4. Register your automobile(s) and obtain a Florida license plate at the tax collector's office in the county where you reside. To accomplish this, you should drive the automobile

you are registering to the tax collector's office because a tax official must physically inspect the automobile's serial number. Alternatively, if your car is located in another state, some Florida counties will provide a form that can be used to verify your vehicle's serial number by certain officials (i.e., police officer) in other jurisdictions. For more information, see Chapters 7 and 9.

5. Apply for your homestead exemption. This should be done at the property appraiser's office in the county where your home is located. At peak times of the year, there may be other designated locations in your county where you may apply, such as a booth at your local mall. For a list of the items you will need to bring when applying for a Florida homestead exemption, see Chapters 3 and 5. To be prudent, if you are married and both spouses own the homestead jointly, both spouses should file the homestead application. A sample homestead exemption application (Form DR 501) is included in Appendix B2.

"Harold, your right turn signal is still 'on'."

If GM had kept up with technology like the computer industry has, we would all be driving $25 cars that got 1,000 mpg.
– Bill Gates

CHAPTER 7

FLORIDA DRIVER LICENSES AND MOTOR VEHICLES

To make your move to Florida complete, you will need to obtain a driver license, register your vehicles and obtain the necessary insurance. There are 129 Tax Collector offices in 46 Florida counties that offer driver license services. By reviewing the steps below, you will find these tasks relatively straightforward to accomplish.

Driver License

If you move to Florida and intend to drive, you must get a Florida driver license within thirty days of becoming a resident. For this purpose, you are considered a resident of Florida if you do any of the following:

- File a Florida declaration of domicile.
- Enroll your children in a Florida public school.
- Register to vote in Florida.
- File for a Florida homestead exemption.
- Accept employment in Florida.
- Reside in Florida for more than six consecutive months.

You do not need a Florida driver license if you have a valid driver license from another state or country and you are:

- A nonresident visitor who is at least sixteen years old.
- A nonresident attending college in Florida.
- Employed by the U.S. government and drive a U.S. government motor vehicle on official business.
- A nonresident working in Florida under a contract for the U.S. government (note: this exemption is valid for sixty days).
- A person who drives only temporarily on the highway (i.e., farm equipment).
- A licensed driver who lives in another state and travels regularly between his or her home and Florida workplace.
- A nonresident migrant farm worker who has a valid license from his or her home state. This is true even if the nonresident migrant farm worker has children in a Florida public school.

If you are a member of the Armed Forces stationed in Florida, you will not need a Florida license except under the following circumstances:

- You or your spouse claims a Florida homestead exemption. In this case, all the drivers in your family must obtain Florida licenses.
- You become employed in Florida. All the drivers in your family must each obtain a Florida driver license.
- Your spouse becomes employed in Florida. Your spouse and children who drive must obtain Florida licenses.
- One or more of your children becomes employed. Only the employed child who drives must obtain a Florida license.

To obtain a Florida driver license or identification (ID) card, you will be required to provide a driver license from another state or country, a certified copy of your birth certificate or passport and social security number (if issued) to a Florida driver license office.

These requirements apply to immigrants as well as nonimmigrants.

If you have an out-of-state license, you may be able to convert your license without taking a written or road test. You will need to have a vision test—so bring along your glasses or wear your contacts if you need them for driving. Some local driver license offices will allow you to call ahead and schedule an appointment. To locate the nearest driver license office, call the Customer Service Center (statewide) at 850-617-2000 or find the local phone number online at www.hsmv.state.fl.us/offices.

Florida Identification (ID) Card

If you do not drive, you can obtain a Florida identification card at any Florida driver license office. If you are sixty years of age or older, the card is good for life; otherwise, it is valid for four years. Similar to a Florida driver license, the ID card will contain such things as your name, address, date of birth and color photograph. To obtain the ID card, you must meet the following criteria:

- Be five years of age or older and have a Social Security number. (Note that certain counties have no minimum age requirement and any person can be issued an identification card if applying for a disabled parking permit.).
- Present your official Social Security card (issued by the Social Security Administration).
- Present one other form of identification (e.g., either an original or a certified copy of a passport or birth certificate).

Canadian Citizens

Under federal law, Canadian citizens are nonimmigrants and are allowed to stay in the United States without obtaining U.S. Citizenship and Immigration Services (CIS) documentation. Canadians without such documentation must provide proof of Canadian citizenship to be issued a Florida driver license or identification card by presenting any two of the following:

- Canadian driver license,
- Original or certified copy of the Canadian birth certificate,
- Canadian passport, and/or
- Canadian naturalization certificate.

If you are not a Canadian citizen but have a Canadian driver license, you are required to provide the same proof of legal presence as any other non-U.S. citizen.

First Time Drivers

If you are seeking a Florida driver license and have never been issued a license in any state or country, you will be required to complete a traffic law and substance abuse education course as a prerequisite for obtaining a Florida driver license.

There are various course options available to satisfy the substance abuse education requirement, including an online course offered in association with the American Safety Council at www. firsttimedriver.com.

THE PREFERRED TOURIST DESTINATION

According to VISIT FLORIDA®, the official tourism marketing corporation for the State of Florida, 20.8 million travelers visited the Sunshine State during the second quarter of 2010 (April - June).

Tourism from within the United States climbed 2.4 percent, while overseas visitors increased by 11.9 percent.

Source: visitflorida.org.

Changes to Your Driver License

If your address or name changes, you have to obtain a new license showing your new address or name change within ten days of that change. Be sure to bring a court order or marriage license to the Florida driver license office for proof of any name change.

If you are an immigrant and have legally changed your name by marriage or court order, you must have your name changed on your U.S. Citizenship and Immigration Services (CIS) documents. A receipt from CIS indicating Form I-90 has been filed for a name change is acceptable for a name change on your driver license or identification card.

If you are Canadian and have legally changed your name by marriage or court order, you must have your name changed on your Canadian license and/or passport before applying for a name change on your Florida driver license or identification card.

Renewals, Duplicates or Replacements

Any immigrant or nonimmigrant holding a Florida driver license or identification card who needs a renewal, duplicate or replacement driver license or identification card must apply in person at a driver license office and present his or her identification documents as described above.

A ROAD TO PARADISE

Road construction in Florida did not take off until the 1940s. The most impressive project from that era was the Overseas Highway, which was a network of roads, bridges and ferries connecting Key West to mainland Florida. Today, Keys visitors can drive all the way from Miami to Key West's famous Duval Street, with no ferries needed.

Source: Florida Department of Transportation.

Additional Information

The Florida Department of Highway Safety and Motor Vehicles made $2 billion for fiscal year 2009/2010 from fees, fines and titles. Additional information about the agency can be found at www. hsmv.state.fl.us.

Motor Vehicle Insurance Laws

Florida Law requires you to have motor vehicle insurance that meets the following criteria:

- Your insurance must be written as Florida coverage.
- Whichever company issues your Florida policy must be an insurance company licensed by the Florida Office of Insurance Regulation.
- Any person who has a motor vehicle in Florida for more than 90 days (consecutive or not) during a 365-day period must be covered under a personal injury protection and property damage liability insurance policy.

You must maintain the required minimum coverage (see the sections "Financial Responsibility Law" and "No-Fault Law," below) at all times for the vehicles you register.

BETTER ID FOR FLORIDA DRIVERS

The Florida Department of Transportation has put into place new procedures and enhanced security measures to confirm the identities of applicants and comply with federal regulations that will provide Florida residents with a more secure and reliable form of personal identification. Plus, over 20 percent of Florida driver license and identification card holders have participated in a new online registration process that allows them to list their emergency contact information with the Department. Add your emergency contact information at: https://www8.flhsmv.gov/eci/

To protect its citizens, Florida has two important insurance laws: the financial responsibility law and the no-fault law. You should understand these laws because, unless you have the proper insurance, you could lose your driver license and vehicle registration tag and may have to pay substantial fees to have them reinstated.

Financial Responsibility Law (FRL) requires owners and operators of motor vehicles to be financially responsible for damages and/or injuries they may cause to others when a motor vehicle accident happens in Florida. The FRL requires any licensed person to have either the following minimum liability insurance or to post a bond or cash that guarantees responsibility for the following minimum limits:

- $10,000 bodily injury liability (BIL)
- $20,000 bodily injury liability to two or more persons
- $10,000 property damage liability (PDL)
- $30,000 combined single limits

The above is often referred to as the 10/20/10 requirements and there are penalties if there is an accident and the vehicle operator does not meet these minimums. The penalties include the suspension of the driver license of the operator and the registrations of all vehicles of the owner.

If you are involved in any of the following violations and you do not have insurance that complies with the FRL, your driver license and/ or vehicle registration tag can be suspended for up to three years:

- A crash where you were at fault;
- A suspension for too many points against your driver license;
- A citation for driving under the influence (DUI) of alcohol, which results in a revocation;
- A revocation for being a "habitual traffic offender;"
- A revocation for any serious offense where the Florida Department of Highway Safety and Motor Vehicles is required to revoke your license.

In addition, if you are the driver or the owner of a vehicle which is in a crash that is your fault, the Florida Department of Highway Safety and Motor Vehicles may require you to pay for some or all of the damages before your driving privileges are reinstated.

The No-Fault Law requires anyone who owns or has registered a motor vehicle with four or more wheels (excluding limousines and taxis) that has been in the state for 90 days or more (consecutive or not) during the past 365 days to have a Florida insurance policy with the following minimum coverages:

- $10,000 of personal injury protection (PIP)
- $10,000 of property damage liability (PDL)

Proper Florida insurance coverage, based on the above laws, is necessary before you will be able to register your car or other four-wheel vehicle. In addition, your insurance company must notify the Department of Highway Safety and Motor Vehicles if you renew, fail to renew or cancel your Florida policy.

In other words, you must maintain Florida insurance coverage the entire time your vehicle is registered in your name. You must turn in the registration and license tag at any Florida Driver License Office or the Department of Highway Safety and Motor Vehicles (via mail) if you cancel the insurance, place the vehicle in storage or if the vehicle is not in working order.

Proof of Insurance

Insurance companies licensed to do business in Florida will issue you an insurance certificate or ID card. You must have this certificate or ID card ready to show to any police officer to prove that you have the required insurance. If not, you may be ticketed for not having proof of insurance.

Alternatively, you may obtain a "self-insurance certificate" from the Bureau of Financial Responsibility by either depositing cash or securities with the department or by providing satisfactory proof of financial responsibility.

Insurance Types

The typical motor vehicle insurance policy has several separate components.

Personal injury protection (PIP) compensates for a loss regardless of who is charged with causing the automobile accident. PIP applies to bodily injury to you, relatives who live in your home, other passengers of your vehicle and licensed drivers who drive your vehicle with your permission. PIP insurance also protects you if you are injured as a pedestrian or bicyclist as long as the injury is caused by a motor vehicle.

Bodily injury liability (BIL) pays for serious injury or death to others when you or a member of your family who lives with you causes an accident involving your or someone else's automobile. Your insurance company will pay for injuries up to the limits of your policy and provide legal representation for you if you get sued. It may also cover others who drive your automobile with your permission.

The purchase of BIL is optional if you post a bond or cash that guarantees responsibility for the 10/20/10 limits. However, if you have been convicted of certain driving offenses and/or have been in an accident, you may be required to purchase BIL coverage.

Property damage liability (PDL) pays for damages to other people's property for which you or members of your family are liable in a crash involving a motor vehicle.

Factors Affecting Personal Insurance Rates

Motor vehicle insurance rates in Florida can be affected by a number of factors:

FLORIDA'S TOP 10 SALTWATER GAME FISH

Saltwater fishing is an all-time favorite for both residents and travelers alike. The miles of coastline make saltwater fishing a family sport or an individual leisure activity. Florida's top ten saltwater game fish, their size and seasons are:

Redfish: 18 to 27 inches; no closed season

Sea Trout: 24 to 34 inches; season depends on location

Snook: 24 to 34 inches; closed season of December 15 to January 31 and June 1 to August 31

Tarpon: No minimum size limit; no closed season

Sailfish: 57-inch minimum size; no closed season

Dolphin: No minimum size limit; no closed season

Grouper: 20-inch minimum size; no closed season

Snapper: Size depends on species; no closed season

Cobia: 33-inch minimum size; no closed season

King Mackerel: 20-inch minimum size; no closed season

Note: Licenses are required for recreational fishing except on some piers, so check before you start casting.

Source: fishingcapital.com.

Sailfish

- Your age and gender.
- Your driving history.
- The type and age of automobile you drive.
- The value of the automobile you drive.
- The existence of antitheft devices on your vehicle.
- The distance you drive to work.
- The number of years you have had your driver license.
- The existence of safety devices on your vehicle.
- The geographic area in which the automobile will be used.

Information Sources

For additional insurance information, such as a list of insurance companies licensed to do business in Florida and motor vehicle requirements, contact:

Office of Insurance Regulation at 850-413-3140. Florida Department of Highway Safety and Motor Vehicles online at www. hsmv.state.fl.us

VEHICLES

Titling a Motor Vehicle in Florida

To title your motor vehicle in Florida, you have to complete an application for certificate of title that is available at any office of the Department of Highway Safety and Motor Vehicles. Alternatively, you may obtain the application online at www.hsmv.state.fl.us. After getting and completing the form, mail it and your proof of insurance to your local county tax collector office or license plate agency.

If a vehicle is in joint ownership with "and" or "or" between the two names, both signatures are required on the application for Florida title.

When the title is held by a lien holder in a different state, the local tax collector's office will assist you in getting the original sent to Florida. After the Florida title is issued with the recorded lien, it will be returned to the lien holder. A list of Florida tax collectors is at www.dor.myflorida.com/dor/property/taxcollectors.html.

Before a Florida title can be issued, the vehicle identification number (VIN) of the vehicle must be verified. The VIN can be verified by one of the following people on Form HSMV 82042:

- A county tax collector employee or Division of Motor Vehicle compliance examiner.
- A law enforcement officer from any state.
- A licensed dealer from Florida.
- A provost marshal or commissioned officer in active military service, with a rank of second lieutenant or higher.
- A Florida notary.

Form HSMV 82042 must be completed and signed by the vehicle owner and the person performing the VIN verification. The form is available from your local tax collector's office or the Web site of the Florida Department of Highway Safety and Motor Vehicles.

To expedite the process of retitling and registering your out-of-state vehicle in Florida, drive your vehicle and bring your proof of insurance to any office of the Department of Highway Safety and Motor Vehicles. As part of the process, a department employee will accompany you to your vehicle to verify the VIN.

Following is a list of vehicles exempt from VIN verification:

- New vehicles when a manufacturer's certificate of origin is submitted (regardless whether purchased in or out of Florida).
- Mobile homes.
- Trailers or semitrailers with a net weight of less than 2,000 lbs.
- Travel trailers.
- Camp trailers.
- Truck campers.
- Fifth-wheel recreation trailers.

Registering Motor Vehicles

In Florida, a motor vehicle is required by law to be registered within ten days of the owner either becoming employed, placing children in public school or establishing residency.

Unless a motor vehicle is exempt from titling (such as mopeds, motorized bicycles and trailers weighing less than 2,000 pounds), it must be titled in Florida at the same time it is registered. Both actions can be accomplished by completing an application for certificate of title and registration, as noted above, and submitting the documents by mail or in person at the local county tax collector's office or license plate agency. When you do, you have to submit the original title and proof of Florida insurance. If not taken care of previously, the verification of the VIN can be done at this time by a county tax collector employee.

Registration is for a twelve-month period, which begins the first day of the owner's birth month. Company-owned vehicles use the month of June. The full amount of the registration fee is charged for

HOME OF THE SMALLEST

Florida is home to both the smallest police station and the smallest post office in the United States.

The smallest post office is located in Ochopee and is a designated tourist attraction. After a fire in 1953 destroyed the existing post office, postal workers moved into the tool shed behind the office as a temporary spot. The tiny building serves 1,500 local residents, of which about 900 are American Indians.

The smallest existing police station is in a phone booth in Carrabelle. Originally, since the town was small, there was no need for a station, just a phone on the outside of a building. The booth was created in 1963 to help officers get out of the rain.

the registration period regardless of when, during the registration period, the vehicle is registered. When your vehicle is registered, Florida law requires the registration certificate or an official copy to be in the possession of the operator of the motor vehicle or carried in the vehicle at all times. You must be able to produce this for law enforcement personnel upon demand. If you fail to have this certificate or if your certificate is out of date, you may be ticketed.

Vehicle Transfer Tax

Florida's six percent use tax is due on any vehicle owned less than six months with an out-of-state title that is then brought into Florida. If you purchased a vehicle outside Florida and bring it into Florida within six months, a credit is permitted against your Florida tax obligation for the amount of any tax paid on the purchase in another state. However, Florida does not credit any tax paid to another country. Thus, if the vehicle is purchased in another country, the full amount of use tax (6 percent) applies and is due. It does not matter if the motor vehicle was used in that country for a period of six months or more prior to the time it is brought into Florida.

Miscellaneous Information

Other Services: The office of Florida Motor Vehicle Services/ County Tax Collector can help you with registration, tag, and title for trailers, watercraft and mobile homes. Also, the county tax collector can issue specialty tags and disability parking permits.

SunPass: SunPass is Florida's statewide prepaid toll program for use on most Florida toll roads. SunPass can save you time and money and eliminate your wait at Florida toll plazas. Registration information can be located online at www.sunpass.com.

Driver Records and Privacy Issues: Most Florida motor vehicle and driver license records are subject to public disclosure. The Driver Privacy Protection Act allows you to keep your personal information private by limiting access to this information.

Additional information is online at www.hsmv.state.fl.us/ddl/ DPPAInfo.html. Topics include driver licenses, vehicle tags and registration, insurance issues and traffic school.

FESTIVAL FLORIDA

Whatever your interest, Florida has a popular event to match it. Here are some of the standouts.

Bike Week/Biketoberfest: Every spring and fall, motorcycle enthusiasts congregate in Daytona Beach to celebrate the biking culture.

Florida Folk Festival: Over its fifty-five-year history, the Florida Folk Festival has celebrated the best of folk music with some of its biggest names. Held in the Stephen Foster Folk Culture Center State Park, it is one of America's largest and oldest folk festivals.

Pirate Festivals: Several cities, including Tampa's famous Gasparilla Pirate Invasion in January, Clearwater and Key West, host swashbuckling weekends complete with tall ships, parades, marathons, costumes and piratical reenactments.

Film Festivals: Becoming increasingly popular are boutique film festivals around Florida. Most feature up-and-coming filmmakers and typically include several dinner or special screening events. Attend one in Sarasota, Naples, Orlando or Fort Lauderdale.

Florida Seafood Festival: For over forty years, delectable seafood and local crafts have welcomed visitors to this Apalachicola tradition. A parade, oyster eating and shucking contests and the blessing of the fishing fleet highlight this delicious weekend.

Florida Strawberry Festival: Plant City in central Florida is at the center of the Florida strawberry industry. Since 1930, its famous festival has hosted parades, home cooking, marching bands and crafts, all in celebration of the strawberry.

THE FLORIDA SEA COW

Manatees are a well-known Florida animal. These slow-moving mammals live in both fresh- and saltwater, eating aquatic vegetation. The biggest cause of manatee mortality is motorboat propellers. Too slow to move away, they can be maimed or killed. The well-known manatee-theme Florida license plate helped to raise awareness and protect manatees. Through 2007, nearly $40 million has been collected for the Save the Manatee Trust Fund.

Florida manatees like shallow, slow-moving rivers, bays, estuaries and coastal water ecosystems. They enjoy waters that are about three - seven feet deep. Their habitat provides natural shelter where they enjoy a steady, easily obtainable food supply.

In the winter, manatees seek warmer waters, like springs and warm-water discharges at power plants. That is the best time to see a manatee. Favorite manatee-watching spots include Blue Springs State Park, the Tampa Electric Company (TECO), Lee County Manatee Park and Merritt Island National Wildlife Refuge. Many Florida aquariums also display rehabbing manatees.

Source: myfwc.com, savethemanatee.org.

Reprinted with permission of BigStockPhoto

BOATS

Registration and Title

If you own and operate a motorboat (or any non-motor-powered vessel longer than sixteen feet) on Florida's public waterways, you must register it at the local county tax collector's office.

When you purchase a boat, either new or used, you have thirty days to apply for registration and title through the county tax collector's office. During this grace period, you must keep a bill of sale with proof of the date of purchase aboard the watercraft. Operation of an unregistered vessel after thirty days is a second-degree misdemeanor.

Applications for watercraft registration and title certificates must be filed by the vessel owner with the county tax collector's office either in the county where the watercraft is located or in the county where the vessel owner resides.

Unless a vessel is exempt from titling, it must be titled at the same time it is registered. Both actions can be accomplished by completing Form HSMV 82040 (available from your local tax collector's office). Along with the completed form, a manufacturer's statement of origin, or its equivalent, must be submitted with the applicable registration fees.

GOVERNMENT AT A GLANCE

Number of counties in Florida: 67

Form of government: Governor and independent cabinet consisting of three elected state executives, the attorney general, chief financial officer and commissioner of agriculture

Legislature: 120 House districts, 40 Senate districts, 23 Congressional districts

In addition, if the sales tax on the total purchase price of the vessel has not already been paid, the owner must pay the tax in Florida. If the sales tax has been paid, then the vessel owner must provide the county tax collector with a valid receipt indicating where the sales tax was paid and that it was paid in an amount equal to or greater than the applicable Florida sales tax.

Visitors

It is not necessary to register a watercraft in Florida if it is in Florida for ninety days or less and has a current out-of-state registration.

Vessels Exempt from Registration

- Non-motor-powered vessels
- Vessels used exclusively on private lakes and ponds
- Vessels owned by the U.S. government
- Vessels used exclusively as a ship's lifeboat

Vessels Exempt from Titling

- Non-motor-powered vessels less than 16 feet in length
- Federally documented vessels
- Vessels used exclusively on private lakes and ponds
- Amphibious vessels for which a vehicle title is issued by the Department of Highway Safety and Motor Vehicles
- Vessels used solely for demonstration, testing or sales promotional purposes by a dealer or manufacturer
- Vessels owned and operated by the state or its political subdivisions
- Vessels from a country, other than the Unites States, temporarily using the waters of this state for not more than 90 days
- Vessels already covered by registration numbers awarded according to a federally approved numbering system of another state or by the U.S. Coast Guard in a state without

a federally approved numbering system, provided that the vessels are not operated in Florida waters more than ninety consecutive days

Transfer of Title to a Vessel

Under Florida law you may not sell, assign or transfer a vessel titled in Florida without delivering to the purchaser/transferee a valid certificate of title, verifying transfer to the new owner.

You may not purchase or otherwise acquire a vessel required to be titled by the state without obtaining a certificate of title for it in your name. Florida law requires you, as the purchaser or transferee, to file an application for a title transfer within thirty days with the county tax collector of the county where the vessel is located or where you, the new owner, reside and pay the required service fees.

When an application for transfer of ownership is filed with the county tax collector, the purchaser or transferce must surrender the last title document issued for the vessel, after it has been properly executed, to the county tax collector. In addition, the new owner

SO CLOSE TO CUBA

Key West is home of the southernmost point of the continental United States. Here you will find mile marker 0, which is in the shape of a buoy. From that point, Cuba is only 90 miles away.

Reprinted with permission of BigStockPhoto

must pay the applicable sales tax on the total purchase price or provide proof of sales tax payment. For answers to other questions or for specific instructions regarding the transfer of ownership based on other factors, such as prior federal documentation, probate or contractual default, contact your local Florida county tax collector's office.

Registration Number

The Florida registration number issued to a vessel is permanent and remains with the vessel as long as it is operated or stored in Florida. This is true even if the vessel is sold or transferred.

The registration number issued to an undocumented vessel must be painted or permanently attached to both sides of the bow (front half) of the vessel and must be in block letters and numerals at least 3 inches high. The registration number must read from left to right, must contrast in color with the hull and be maintained in legible condition.

The prefix and suffix must be separated from the numerals by a space equal to the width of the digits (e.g., "FL 0008 MK").

SUGARCANE

Sugarcane is a tropical grass that is grown throughout Florida. In most areas of the state, sugarcane is grown only as a hobby crop for syrup production or as a source of "chewing cane." Sugarcane is grown commercially for the production of crystal or "white" sugar primarily along the shores of Lake Okeechobee. Palm Beach County accounts for approximately 70 percent of the commercial sugarcane acreage. The remainder is grown in the adjacent counties of Hendry, Glades and Martin.

Source: Institute of Food and Agriculture, University of Florida.

Decals

A decal signifying the year during which the registration certificate is valid is issued with each registration certificate. The decal must be displayed on the port side of the vessel immediately before or after the registration number. If issued to a federally documented vessel, the decal may be affixed to a window or windshield on the port side. Decals for a previous year's registration must be removed from the vessel.

Out-of-State Registration

Florida recognizes valid registration certificates and numbers issued to visiting vessel owners by other states for 90 days. If you plan to use your vessel in Florida longer than 90 days, you must register it with a county tax collector. However, you may retain the out-of-state registration number if you intend to return to your home state within a reasonable period of time. If you have any questions, check with your county tax collector's office.

Out-of-state vessel owners who plan to remain permanently in Florida must notify the county tax collector. You will then receive a Florida registration certificate number to replace those issued by your former state. The out-of-state registration and certificate of title, if issued, must be surrendered to the tax collector.

Out-of-state registration certificates and numbers for vessels owned by military personnel on active duty in Florida are valid in Florida until the expiration date, after which the vessels must be registered by Florida.

AIRCRAFT

If you own or plan to purchase an airplane or helicopter, there are a few things you should know if you intend to operate and/or store your aircraft in Florida.

Registration

Aircraft operated in Florida must be registered in accordance with the regulations of the Federal Aviation Administration. Florida does not require a separate state registration of aircraft.

Tax Issues

In Florida, tax compliance is an important aspect of aircraft ownership. Tax dollars are used toward airport construction, improvements to runways and various other necessary services to benefit aircraft owners.

Sales Tax

All aircraft sold and/or delivered in Florida are subject to Florida's 6 percent sales tax, unless the transaction is specifically exempt by law, as discussed below. Florida aircraft dealers and brokers are required to collect sales tax from the purchaser at the time of sale or delivery.

If the aircraft is delivered into a county that imposes a discretionary sales surtax, then the dealer or broker must collect this tax. Discretionary sales surtax applies only to the first $5,000 of the aircraft purchase price. All sales of aircraft between individuals are fully taxable if the sale and/or delivery occurs in Florida.

Trade-Ins

If a sale and trade-in are included in a single transaction, the trade-in allowance may be deducted from the selling price. Thus, only the net sales price is subject to Florida sales tax and applicable discretionary surtax.

Use Tax

Use tax is a component of Florida's sales and use tax law which provides uniform taxation of items, such as airplanes, which may be purchased outside Florida but used, hangared or stored in Florida. Use tax is due on purchases made out of the state and brought into Florida within six months of the purchase date.

Aircraft purchased and used outside Florida for more than six months are generally exempt when brought into Florida if the two following conditions are met:

- The owner has owned the aircraft for more than six months, and
- The owner has used the aircraft in another state or states, U.S. territory or District of Columbia for six months or longer prior to bringing the aircraft to Florida.

FLORIDA'S FIRST CITY

You can visit Florida's Spanish roots in St. Augustine, the oldest European settlement in North America. St. Augustine was founded in 1565, forty-two years before the English colony at Jamestown, Virginia, and fifty-five years before the Pilgrims landed on Plymouth Rock in Massachusetts. The Castillo de San Marcos Fort, built in 1672, served primarily as a colony of the Spanish Empire, guarding St. Augustine. The fort has withstood over 300 years of warfare and ocean storms.

Castillo de San Marcos Tower

Reprinted with permission of BigStockPhoto

Source: oldcity.org.

To report use tax due to Florida on the purchase of an aircraft, the purchaser should complete an ownership declaration and sales and use tax report on aircraft (Form DR-42A). See below for information on obtaining this and other forms.

Tax Credits for Purchases Outside Florida

Florida allows credit for sales or use taxes lawfully imposed and paid to another state, U.S. territory or the District of Columbia, if the aircraft later becomes subject to Florida tax.

Florida does not allow credit for taxes paid to a foreign country and will not recognize use in a foreign country for any length of time. Any aircraft imported from a foreign country to Florida for use, distribution or storage (with the intent to be used in Florida) is subject to Florida's use tax.

GEOGRAPHY: NORTHEAST FLORIDA

Florida's northeast boundaries stretch from Jacksonville south to Cape Canaveral. The major cities in northeast Florida are Jacksonville, Daytona Beach and St. Augustine. Surfers and sunbathers alike are drawn to this region's famous beaches. It's even possible to drive on the beach in Daytona Beach. St. Augustine offers historic tours and shopping and is also home to the St. Augustine Alligator Farm where you can see all 23 species of crocodilians on display. The Ron Jon Surf Shop in Cocoa Beach is billed as the largest surf shop in the world. Space enthusiasts might catch a launch at the Kennedy Space Center or experience simulated astronaut training at Cape Canaveral.

Ramp Checks (Visual Inspections)

To ensure that the appropriate tax has been paid on aircraft operated or stored in Florida, the Florida Department of Revenue

FACTS ABOUT NORTHEAST FLORIDA

Saint Augustine (founded in 1565) is the oldest European settlement in North America.

Nearly 80 percent of the U.S. intake of sweet Atlantic white shrimp is harvested in Amelia Island waters. Two million pounds of shrimp are delivered to Fernandina docks annually.

The first graded road built in Florida was Old Kings Road in 1763. It was named for King George of England.

During the 1991 Gulf War, the busiest military port in the country was Jacksonville. From this location, the military moved more supplies and people than from any other port in the country.

When first completed in 1989, the Dames Point Bridge became the longest cable-stayed span in the United States, the longest concrete span of its type in the Western Hemisphere and the third longest cable-stayed bridge in the world.

The longest river sailboat race in the world is the Annual Mug Race. The event runs 42 miles from Palatka to Jacksonville along the St. Johns River.

Titusville, known as Space City, USA, is located on the west shore of the Indian River directly across from the John F. Kennedy Space Center.

Source: www.50states.com/facts/florida.htm.

periodically conducts ramp checks, which are visual inspections at Florida airports and fixed-base operation facilities.

Information and Forms

For detailed responses to your additional concerns and questions, contact:

>Aircraft Enforcement Unit
>Florida Department of Revenue
>PO Box 6417
>Tallahassee, FL 32314-6417
>Telephone: 850-487-3273
>Fax: 850.487.0969
>www.myflorida.com/dor

To speak with a Department of Revenue representative, call Taxpayer Services, Monday through Friday, 8 a.m. to 7 p.m., ET, at 800-352-3671.

Persons with hearing or speech impairments may call the TDD line at 800-367-8331 or 850-922-1115.

Any of the following methods will allow you to receive forms by mail:

Order multiple copies of forms from www.myflorida.com/dor/forms.

Fax form requests to the DOR Distribution Center at 850-922-2208.

Mail form requests to Distribution Center, Florida Department of Revenue, 168A Blountstown Highway, Tallahassee, FL 32304-2702.

NOTES

"Oh yeah? Well, I'm offering a 700 billion dollar tax cut AND a free tote bag!"

*Nobody will ever deprive the American people of the right
to vote except the American people themselves and the only
way they could do this is by not voting.*
— Franklin D. Roosevelt

CHAPTER 8

REGISTERING TO VOTE IN FLORIDA

You may vote in any Florida election that applies to your Florida city or county if you are registered to vote. To register, you must:

- Be a citizen of the United States of America.
- Be a Florida resident.
- Be eighteen years old (you may preregister if you are seventeen).
- Not have been adjudicated mentally incapacitated with respect to voting in Florida or any other state.
- Not have been convicted of a felony without your civil rights having been restored.
- Have a current and valid Florida driver license number or Florida identification card number. If you don't have either, you must provide the last four digits of your Social Security number.

How to Register

You can register to vote at your local county supervisor of elections office. Alternatively, you can register at any Florida driver license office. A driver license examiner will ask you if you would like to apply for voter registration or change your address or party affiliation and provide you with an application of registration at the time you receive your license. Your voter registration application is then forwarded to your local county supervisor of elections office. Your official registration card will be mailed to you by your local county supervisor of elections office.

You may apply for voter registration online by downloading the form at election.dos.state.fl.us/voter-registration/voter-reg. shtml. Simply fill out, print and sign the online Florida voter registration application form. Using the address provided, mail the application to your county supervisor of elections or hand-deliver the signed form to a Florida driver license office, a voter registration agency, an armed forces recruitment office, the Florida Division of Elections or to any Florida office of the supervisor of elections.

The date your completed application is postmarked or hand-delivered to a voter registration agency will be your registration date. You must be registered at least twenty-nine days before you can vote in an election.

PIONEERS IN TRANSPORTATION

Railroad barons helped make Florida what it is today. One of the best-known tycoons was Henry Flagler. A prototypical businessman, real estate investor and partner in Standard Oil, Flagler developed the East Coast Railway after visiting and falling in love with St. Augustine. Like other railroad men, he also built a lavish hotel, the Ponce de León Hotel, to attract tourists.

One of the major Southwest Florida roads is the Tamiami Trail, running from Tampa to Miami. When tourism and industry started to boom in the 1920s, Barron G. Collier helped fund the building and paving of the trail. In return, the State Legislature created Collier County. Tamiami Trail officially opened in 1928. When Collier died in 1939, he was the largest landowner in Florida.

If your application is complete and you qualify as a voter, the supervisor of elections will mail you a voter information card. You may call your county supervisor of elections if you have not received your card within eight weeks or if you have any questions.

Florida is a closed primary state. If you wish to register to vote in a partisan primary election, you must be a registered voter in the party for which the primary is being held. Your Florida application form has a place to make your party preference known. All registered voters, regardless of party affiliation, can vote on all ballot questions and issues and for all nonpartisan candidates. Begin the voting process online and:

- Register to vote in the State of Florida,
- Change your name or address,
- Replace your defaced, lost or stolen voter registration card,
- Register with a political party or change party affiliation,
- Update your signature.

BUMP INTO VANITY

Florida helped to start the specialty license plate craze in 1986 when it issued a commemorative plate of the space shuttle Challenger. Since then, Florida has developed over one hundred theme plates, which support various causes from universities and conservation to sports teams and charities.

One of the most popular Florida specialty plates is the "Protect the Panther" plate. Since its creation in 1990, over 1.4 million plates have been issued and over $42 million has been raised for panther research and conservation.

*Patience is something you admire in the driver behind you
and scorn in the one ahead.*
– Mac McCleary

CHAPTER 9

PART 2: QUESTIONS AND ANSWERS
HOW TO ESTABLISH FLORIDA DOMICILE

Vehicle Registration

Q: What is a registration?

A: A registration is evidence of having paid the registration tax and fees on a motor vehicle. It consists of a metal license plate, a validation decal and a registration certificate.

Q: Why must I register my motor vehicle?

A: In the state of Florida, a motor vehicle is required by law to be registered within ten days of the owner becoming employed, placing children in public school or establishing residency. Registering your motor vehicle goes hand in hand with the titling process.

Q: How do I register a vehicle if I am out of state?

A: If registering a vehicle from out of state, complete the application for certificate of title. Mail the completed form and fee to your local Florida county tax collector or license plate agency.

Q: How do I register a vehicle if I am in Florida?

A: If registering a vehicle in person, submit the original title and proof of Florida insurance to the local county tax collector or license plate agency.

Q: What are the basic registration fees?

A: Registration rates, subject to statutory change, are shown in the following table.

Classification	Weight	Annual Tax & Other Fees
Automobiles (private use)	up to 2499 lbs.	$19.50
	2500 - 3499 lbs.	$30.50
	3500 lbs. or greater	$44.00
Trucks (private & commercial)	up to 1999 lbs.	$19.50
	2000 - 3000 lbs.	$30.50
	3001 - 5000 lbs.	$44.00

For registration fees for motorcycles, mopeds, mobile homes, trailers and others, call your local tax collector's office or go online at dor.myflorida.com/dor/property/taxcollectors.html.

Q: If I don't register my vehicle on time, is there a delinquent fee?

A: Section 320.07(4)(a), Florida Statutes, specifically requires the delinquent fee to be imposed on any applicant who fails to renew a registration before the end of the month in which renewal registration is due.

The delinquent fee is applied beginning on the eleventh calendar day of the month succeeding the renewal period. The exact expiration date is shown on the current registration certificate. Therefore, the registered owner should be well aware of when his or her registration expires.

Q: Why must out-of-state residents have Florida proof of insurance before obtaining a license plate or registration renewal?

A: Florida insurance is required to meet the requirements of Florida statutes. Only insurance issued or countersigned by a Florida agent is electronically reported to the Department of Highway Safety and Motor Vehicles for verification purposes.

Q: Do I have to change the name on my registration when I marry or divorce?

A: Your name can be changed in the Florida Motor Vehicle Services/County Tax Collector database after your driver license has been changed. This will change your name on the registration; however, the printed title will still have your previous name unless you apply for a new title. If there is a lien on the vehicle, the lien holder may not allow a new title to be printed. It is permissible to leave the name unchanged on the printed title because the owner is still the same person.

Q: Do I carry the registration on me or in the car?

A: Section 320.0605, Florida Statutes, requires the registration certificate or an official copy to be in the possession of the operator of the motor vehicle or carried in the vehicle at all times. Therefore, either way is permissible as long as a copy can be produced for law enforcement upon demand.

Q: What is required to register my motorcycle, scooter or moped?

A: Information for registering motorcycles, scooters and mopeds is contained in the DMV Procedures Manual, procedure number RS-61. For registration fees for motorcycles and mopeds, it is best to contact your local driver license office.

QUESTIONS AND ANSWERS

Title

Q: What is a title?

A: A certificate of title is the proof of ownership of a motor vehicle in the state of Florida. Most vehicles are required to be

GEOGRAPHY: SOUTHWEST FLORIDA

Southwest Florida runs from Tampa south to Everglades City. The major cities in southwest Florida are Tampa, Sarasota, Fort Myers and Naples. On the gulf coast of Florida, superb white sand beaches and resort hotels abound. The beaches in Sarasota and Fort Myers Beach are especially attractive. Sanibel Island and Siesta Key are a mix of the quaint and sophisticated, where visitors can buy from local artists and enjoy fine dining. Inland, Corkscrew Swamp and Six-Mile Cypress Preserve are home to ancient cypress trees. In Tampa, families enjoy Busch Gardens, the Florida Aquarium and Sunken Gardens. Ybor City, the city's Spanish and Cuban district, offers Latin food and culture.

titled. The exceptions are mopeds, motorized bicycles and trailers weighing less than 2,000 pounds.

Q: When must I apply for title?

A: When, as a Florida resident, you purchase a new motor vehicle, or bring one into the state or change the ownership, you must apply for a title in your name.

Q: What do I need as proper proof of insurance?

A: Proof of personal injury protection (PIP) and property damage liability (PDL) insurance may be shown using the original

FACTS ABOUT SOUTHWEST FLORIDA

The name Punta Gorda means "fat point" in Spanish. The moniker was given to the city because a broad part of the land in Punta Gorda juts into Charlotte Harbor.

A museum in Sanibel owns two million shells and claims to be the world's only museum devoted solely to mollusks.

Safety Harbor is the home of the historic Espiritu Santo Springs, named in 1539 by the Spanish explorer Hernando DeSoto. The natural springs have attracted attention worldwide for their curative powers.

Venice is known as the Shark Tooth Capital of the World. Collecting prehistoric sharks' teeth has been a favorite pastime of visitors and residents of the Venice area for years.

Ybor City was once known as the Cigar Capital of the World. With nearly 12,000 tabaqueros (cigar makers) employed in 200 factories, it produced about 700 million cigars a year at the industry's peak.

or a photocopy of one of the following:

- Florida automobile insurance identification card,
- Florida insurance policy,
- Certificate of insurance or
- An original affidavit signed by the insured, giving the name of the insurance company, policy number, type of insurance coverage and the description of the vehicle.

Q: What must I have to apply for registration and title?

A: You must have proof of ownership and proof of required insurance coverage written or countersigned by a Florida agent. Next, you must purchase or transfer your license plate. Be sure to record a lien if the vehicle is financed. Then you have to complete and sign the appropriate title application form and pay sales tax, title and registration fees.

Q: Where can I apply for registration and title?

A: Application for registration and title to a motor vehicle can be made at any of the tax collector or license plate agencies located in each of the counties throughout Florida.

Q: If the vehicle is purchased by joint ownership, why do both parties have to be present? Can I sign for my spouse?

A: If a vehicle is purchased by joint ownership with "and" or "or" between the two names, both signatures are required on the application for Florida title, per Section 319.22, Florida Statutes.

Q: Why is sales tax collected if the vehicle has been owned less than six months on an out-of-state title?

A: Florida state law requires that sales tax be collected in Florida for a vehicle owned less than six months on an out-of-state title. The money is actually collected as "use" tax instead of sales tax.

QUESTIONS AND ANSWERS

Voting

Q: How can I find out if I am eligible or registered to vote?

A: If you are uncertain, you can contact your county supervisor of elections to see if you are eligible to vote or to register to vote. You can find contact information for your county supervisor of elections by visiting the Florida Department of State, Division of Elections Web site at election.dos.state.fl.us/SOE/supervisor_elections.shtml. Click on the link for your county for additional information about voter registration, campaigns and elected officials in your county.

WINGED MIGRATION

If you're feeling a little birdbrained, you are not alone. Visitors flock to Florida to see the Great Florida Birding Trail (GFBT), over 446 sites throughout the state, that have been singled out for their outstanding birding opportunities. Florida is home to countless species, from colorful warblers and graceful wading birds to the majestic bald eagle. GFBT maps and guides make it easy to observe some of Florida's distinctive birds.

Birding is more than just a hobby in Florida. Birders boost local economies when they visit their favorite spots. Florida ranks second in the nation, behind only California, for retail sales generated by nonconsumptive bird use. Statewide, it's estimated that birding generates $447 million in retail sales a year.

Source: www.floridabirdingtrail.com.

Q: How do I register to vote?

A: Information about registering to vote and the Florida voter registration application may be accessed on the Florida Division of Election's Web site at election.dos.state.fl.us/voter-registration/voter-reg.shtml. Download the form, print it out and mail it to your county supervisor of elections. The form must include an original signature.

You can also contact your county supervisor of elections office to register to vote. You can find contact information for your county supervisor of elections by visiting the Division of Elections Web site at election.dos.state.fl.us/SOE/supervisor_elections.shtml.

THOSE BEAUTIFUL TREES

Florida is home to hundreds of different species of trees. But, the palm tree is what most people associate with Florida. The royal palm can be recognized by its straight, silver-white trunk. Other palms found in Florida include the sabal palm, also known as the cabbage palm, and the coconut palm, which resembles the royal palm, but is thinner and adorned at the top with the distinctive coconut.

Another favorite tree, the gumbo limbo, takes its nickname, "the tourist tree," from its unique bark. Like visitors who have spent a long day at the beach, this tree's "skin" is also red and peeling.

Florida is home to cypress trees that grow in wet places along rivers, streams and creeks, as well as in swamps with slow moving water. A cypress can live up to 600 years. It is typically draped with Spanish moss and conspicuous for its cypress "knees" – buttresses from the tree that stick out of the water.

Live oaks can be found throughout the state. It is a familiar tree of massive size and density, weighing 55 pounds per cubic foot. Its acorns are a food source to many animals.

Up and down Florida's southern coastline you can find mangroves. These trees are remarkable in their ability to survive in salt water by a process of natural desalination.  The three main species of mangrove—the red mangrove, the white mangrove and the black mangrove—are hosts to many small marine animals and birds and are protected by many laws and regulations.

Reprinted with permission of BigStockPhoto

"I'D LIKE YOU TO ENDORSE MY LIFESTYLE."

PART 3

THE FLORIDA LIFESTYLE

The Florida lifestyle is a celebration of leisure, culture, recreation and entertainment. For many Floridians, home is where there is plenty of sand between the toes and lots of tees between the greens.

But that's not all. From gulfside fishing villages that open and close with the tides to vibrant cities filled with cosmopolitan flair, Florida provides plenty of variety for anyone in search of the good life.

Home sales in Florida continue to rise as buyers continue to relocate in search of a sound investment and a desirable home. And waiting for them are world-class amenities, spectacular beaches, outstanding cultural centers, state-of-the-art medical facilities, quality schools and universities, fine dining, abundant shopping and a wealth of recreational opportunities for a lifestyle beyond compare in a location beyond all expectations.

It's tangible, it's solid, it's beautiful. It's artistic, from my
standpoint, and I just love real estate.
– Donald Trump

CHAPTER 10

PURCHASING A HOME IN FLORIDA

If you are contemplating purchasing a Florida residence, pick up a local Florida newspaper, especially the Sunday edition, and drive around looking at property in the area where you have decided you want to live. After you get serious about home ownership, your next best move is to contact a qualified Realtor who specializes in residential real estate.

Any person who is properly licensed in Florida can sell Florida real estate. However, the term Realtor refers to someone who also subscribes to the strict Code of Ethics of the National Association of Realtors and has access to the Realtor Multiple Listing Service (MLS). The MLS provides current and historical information on properties that have been placed on the market by all Realtors in the area covered by the local board of Realtors. In addition to the strict code of ethics and the MLS, there are continuing educational requirements that separate a Realtor from a salesperson who is simply licensed under a Florida real estate broker.

The National Association of Realtors, in conjunction with local boards of Realtors, offers educational courses to their members that lead to various designations, such as Certified Residential Specialist (CRS) and Graduate Realtors Institute (GRI). These designations, if earned, show a Realtor's commitment to his or her profession as well as an added degree of knowledge about the Realtor's chosen specialty.

One of the biggest advantages of working with a qualified Florida Realtor is their knowledge of the local area, including proximity to schools, shopping, recreation and new planned developments. In addition, the MLS can provide substantial information on properties that are on the market in the area you have selected, thereby saving you a great deal of time and energy. Most MLS systems are computerized, so you or your Realtor will be able to access a large amount of information, often including pictures, through the Internet.

Most real estate professionals in Florida make their living via commissions from the sale of real estate. The commission is usually paid by the seller and, thus, the Realtor owes a fiduciary duty to the seller—to get the highest price. In some circumstances, a Realtor may be hired by a buyer to represent the buyer's interest —to get the most favorable deal for the buyer. In such a case, the buyer would arrange to pay the Realtor to find the "right" property at the lowest price. Some Realtors specialize in representing buyers and, typically, call themselves a "buyer's broker." Before you sign any realty agreements, ascertain for whom the Realtor is working. Whether you use the seller's

KEY DEER

Florida is home to the world's smallest white-tailed deer, the Key deer. Found only in the Florida Keys, they stand less than 3 feet at the shoulder and weigh from 60 to 80 pounds. The Key Deer Wildlife Refuge on Big Pine Key is an ideal place to view this tiny endangered species.

Reprinted with permission of BigStockPhoto

Source: myfwc.com.

Realtor or hire your own, you will benefit from their knowledge, integrity and professionalism.

Negotiating

After locating the home of your choice, the next step is to have your Realtor negotiate an agreement, in writing, with the seller of the property. The local board of Realtors supplies Realtors with a "standard" sales agreement, which you can use to make an offer to a seller. These contracts are carefully designed to cover most of the important items needed to be considered when purchasing and selling a parcel of real estate. However, it may be wise to employ a Florida real estate attorney to ensure that all the bases have been covered and your interests are fully protected. You may want to hire a civil engineer or other qualified property inspector to ensure that the home meets all the applicable building codes and does not have any major defects.

One option is to make an offer that is subject to review by your Florida attorney, so that the terms will not be final until your attorney has reviewed the contract and made any additions, corrections and so forth, to protect your best interest.

Typically, the buyer provides a deposit with an offer to show that the offer is made in "earnest." There is no standard amount for a deposit, but five to ten percent of the purchase price is not uncommon. Often the amount is small (e.g., one percent) until the offer is accepted.

Financing

Most standard Realtor sales contracts include a section that calls for the agreement to be contingent upon the purchaser's success in obtaining financing. Unless you are paying cash for the property, you should fill out that section. You should be sure to give your mortgage lender enough time to complete the approval process, which usually includes an appraisal, survey and so forth.

There are numerous sources in Florida for obtaining real estate loans, including banks, mortgage companies, mortgage brokers and private lenders. It is generally a good idea to deal with a lender that offers a variety of financing choices (such as conventional fixed-rate mortgages, adjustable-rate mortgages, and interest-only mortgages) and one that will be able to make a firm commitment to provide the funds in a specified period of time and stick to the rate quoted to you.

Transfer of Title from an Estate

If the property is passing from an estate, legal and tax issues can easily foul up the timing of the sale and/or closing. The Internal Revenue Service (IRS) and Florida Department of Revenue (DOR) have automatic unwritten estate tax liens on all properties owned by a decedent at the time of death. The tax liens must be cleared to convey clear title to the new owner (either by sale or by inheritance). Depending on the size of the decedent-owner's taxable estate, the method and timing of the clearance of the liens will be different. You should consult a legal adviser who is competent in these matters if you plan to purchase a home from a Florida estate.

Title Insurance

To ensure that you are getting proper title—free from all encumbrances—from the seller, have your attorney examine the title and give you a written opinion. Alternatively, your Florida attorney or a title insurance company can arrange for title insurance to eliminate virtually all title risks. If you are obtaining financing, the mortgage lender will require title insurance, protecting the lender, in the amount of the mortgage. Although the seller is usually required to furnish evidence of title (usually in the form of the seller's title insurance or an abstract that can be recertified to the date of the closing of the sale), the buyer usually pays the premium for the title insurance, including the mortgage title policy. However, in a real estate transaction everything is negotiable, including who pays for the title insurance and amounts paid to real estate professionals for their services.

Closing

The closing is usually scheduled to take place after all the contingencies, such as inspections, have been completed. The closing can be done at the office of the seller's attorney, but is often conducted at the title company furnishing the title insurance or the office of the mortgage lender, if any is involved. In Florida, it is not necessary to have all the parties appear at the closing. In fact, it is not unusual for the buyer to appear without the seller present, as the deed and other papers are often signed in advance by the seller and held in escrow until the buyer has signed and paid the funds for purchase.

The Realtor or the lender should provide a copy of the closing statement—which will list the charges and credits pertaining to the purchase and sale of the real estate—before the closing. Most closing agents will require a certified or cashier's check for the balance of the purchase price plus other closing costs made payable to the trust account of the closing agent. After all the closing papers are signed, including the closing statement, the deed, and any mortgages, the closing agent will disburse the proceeds according to the closing statement and usually takes responsibility

THE SINGING TOWER

Known as the American Taj Mahal, the famous Bok Tower Sanctuary in Lake Wales was erected by Edward W. Bok. The project was started in 1921 as a bird sanctuary and soon grew to be the home of many beautiful gardens, Mr. Bok's estate and a 205-foot tower containing a sixty-bell carillon. Recitals from the carillon are played daily.

Reprinted with permission of bigstockphoto.com

Source: http://boksanctuary.org

for recording the deed in the register of deed's office in the county where the property is located.

Allocating Closing Costs

The costs associated with the purchase of real estate vary, depending on the Florida county in which you are buying. However, in a typical sale in Florida, costs are shared between the buyer and seller, as follows:

The buyer's costs include the following:

- Recording fees associated with requirements under the title insurance commitment,
- Preparation of a purchase money mortgage note to the seller and the documentary stamps and recording fees relating to it,
- All costs, including documentary stamps and recording fees on any institutional loan secured by the buyer,
- Recording condominium/homeowner membership approval,
- Abstract recertification or title continuation through the date of recording of the deed,
- Legal opinion on the title or title insurance (which is often used in lieu of an abstract recertification),
- Survey cost,
- Condominium/homeowner association membership transfer fee,
- Condominium/homeowner association resale transfer fee and any required capital contribution to the association,
- Pending liens or special assessments other than those arising on or before the effective date of the sales agreement unless otherwise covered in the sales agreement,
- Buyer's attorney's fees.

The seller's costs include the following:

- Title evidence or, alternatively, a specified credit to the buyer toward the cost of updated title insurance,
- A current Uniform Commercial Code (UCC) encumbrance search,
- Preparation of warranty deed and other documents such as a bill of sale, assignment of leases, condominium/homeowner association and/or tenant estoppel letters,
- Documentary stamps on the deed of transfer,
- Real estate broker's commission, if applicable,
- Utility services to closing date,
- Condominium/homeowner association special assessment and any government liens or special assessments on or before the effective date of the sales agreement.

Other closing costs that may apply include prorated items and credits for the following:

- Ad valorem and non-ad valorem real and personal property taxes,
- Interest on any assumable indebtedness,
- Rents and security deposits,
- Condominium/homeowner association assessments,
- County waste assessments,
- Appliance service contracts to be assumed by the buyer.

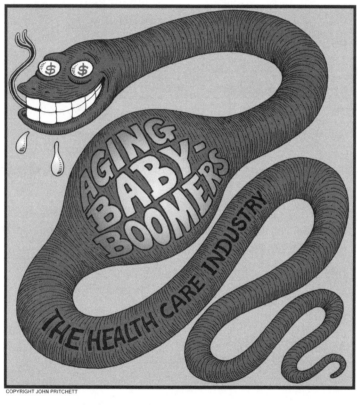

COPYRIGHT JOHN PRITCHETT

Health is like money, we never have a true idea of its value
until we lose it.
– Josh Billings

CHAPTER 11

FLORIDA INSURANCE AND HEALTH CARE OPTIONS

When you become a Florida resident, you should focus on protecting your future by reviewing your insurance coverage. At a minimum, you should check on the benefits of purchasing protection for your home and business. Further, the right type of health maintenance program and insurance coverage will help keep you going strong so you can continue enjoying the benefits of being a Florida resident longer.

Homeowner's Insurance

Although Florida law does not require it, homeowner's insurance can help you in the event of a loss to your home and/or personal property. There are four basic insurance types:

Fire: Fire insurance protects you in the event of a loss to your home and/or personal property from fire and smoke.

Flood: Flood insurance can be particularly important especially if you are located in a flood zone.

Wind: Windstorm coverage protects you in the event of damage to your home and/or personal property from tornadoes, hurricanes, and wind.

Liability: Virtually all homeowners' policies provide liability coverage which pays for non-automobile-related injuries to other persons or their property.

Some cities and counties require you to have liability insurance if you have a swimming pool or own certain pets. In most cases, if you have a mortgage, the lender will require full insurance coverage. Some developers and subdivisions may also require you to maintain liability insurance on your home.

Condominium Owner's Insurance

Under Florida law, condominium associations must provide a minimum standard of insurance coverage. The "association policy" must cover all structures and other common property. You should take the time to examine your association's policy to learn what it covers. The premium for the association policy is typically included in the periodic condominium maintenance fee each homeowner is required to pay.

Condominium Interior Insurance

For the loss protection on that portion of the structure not covered by the association policy, such as your interior wallpaper, trim, built-in book cases, cabinets, fixtures, carpeting, interior liability and so on, and for personal property, you will want to consider purchasing condominium "interior" insurance. Interior policies are separate from the association policy and the additional cost is your responsibility and is not included in your condominium maintenance fees.

Property Insurance for High-Risk Areas

In 2002, the Florida legislature passed a law combining the former Florida Residential Property and Casualty Joint Underwriting Association (FRPCJUA) and the Florida Windstorm Underwriting Association (FWUA). The result was the creation of Citizens Property Insurance Corporation (Citizens), which more efficiently and effectively provides insurance to, and serves the needs of, homeowners in high-risk areas and others who cannot find coverage in the private insurance market. For more information, contact Citizens Property Insurance Corporation at 101 North Monroe Street, Suite 1000, Tallahassee, FL 32301 or online at www.citizensfla.com.

General information regarding homeowner's insurance can be obtained from the Florida Office of Insurance Regulation online at www.floir.com.

Umbrella Policy for Extended Liability Coverage

To add a layer of protection for personal liability against injuries to other persons or property, you should consider purchasing an "umbrella" policy, which typically increases the liability limits of your homeowner's or condominium insurance by an additional amount (e.g., $2 million). Umbrella policies are usually reasonably priced and require you to have base coverage, sometimes with the same insurer, on your Florida home and/or other investment property.

Health Care Programs and Insurance

In the past, Florida has suffered from a reputation as being "God's waiting room." While it is true that many people move to Florida after retirement, Florida boasts a remarkable medical industry that is both cutting edge and competitive. It is home to satellite facilities for the Mayo Clinic and Cleveland Clinic as well as exceptional specialty programs that are making medical history in the areas of fertility, gerontology, heart research and pharmacology.

When asked, most Florida health care providers agree that prevention is the key to success in public health. Being an informed patient includes finding out more about your medical status, your medical conditions, the medical procedures or treatments available and how to get coverage for the appropriate treatment and care.

A RIVER OF GRASS

One of Florida's most recognized features is the Everglades, often called the "river of grass." Historically, the Everglades consisted of a vast network of interconnected wetlands, covering about 8.9 million acres from Orange County to Florida Bay.

Author Marjory Stoneman Douglas played a major role in bringing outside recognition and appreciation to the Everglades. Her classic 1947 book, The Everglades: River of Grass, helped win support for curbing development and draining projects that threatened this unique Florida feature. During the 1950s, sweeping drainage projects diverted or eradicated much of the historic Everglades, affecting Florida's natural water cycle and harming wildlife. The 1994 Everglades Forever Act requires that the Everglades' natural flow be restored and water quality be improved for the benefit of all Florida.

Source: Florida Department of Environmental Protection.

Reprinted with permission of BigStockPhoto

Health Care Assistance

Below are health care programs and assistance available for Florida residents who meet certain income requirements. These programs and services may help if you do not have insurance or if your insurance is not adequate for your needs.

Community Health Centers

Community health centers are federally funded to provide health care in medically underserved areas. To find out if there is a health center in your area and to view a list of services, visit the U.S. Department of Health and Human Services, Health Resources and Services Administration's Web site at www.hrsa.gov.

County Health Departments

Florida county health departments provide some medical services for low cost or no fee depending upon income. To find an office in your area, go to www.doh.state.fl.us/chdsitelist.htm. To find the services available, go to www.doh.state.fl.us/Planning_eval/phealth/services.htm.

Disability Information

The Florida Department of Management Services operates a Clearinghouse on Disabilities that provides information and referrals to state and community programs for disabled persons. Call toll-free 877-232-4968. For a comprehensive federal Web site of disability-related government resources, go to www.disabilityinfo.gov.

Florida Department of Elder Affairs

Florida Department of Elder Affairs (DOEA) offers several community-based programs to assist elders in their homes. Information can be obtained online at www.elderaffairs.state.fl.us or call the Elder Help Line toll-free at 800-963-5337 or TDD 800-955-8771.

National Council on Aging

If you are fifty-five years of age or over, the National Council on Aging has a Web site (www.benefitscheckup.org) with referrals to many programs offering assistance with the cost of medications. It includes information on state-funded programs, state Medicaid programs, and company-sponsored patient assistance programs. You can complete a brief questionnaire online and obtain a report on all the programs you might be eligible for and instructions on how to enroll in them.

Health Flex

Health Flex is a Florida program that encourages health insurers, health maintenance organizations, health care provider-sponsored organizations, local governments, health care districts or other public or private community-sponsored organizations to offer low-cost health insurance options with basic and preventive health care services for low-income, uninsured people who meet various qualifications. The program is not currently available statewide. You may obtain additional information online at www.ahca.myflorida. com/MCHQ/Managed_Health_Care/Health_Flex/index.shtml.

Medicare

Medicare is a federal health insurance program for people who are age sixty-five or older, for disabled persons or for those with end-stage kidney disease. There are four major parts to the Medicare program:

Part A: Hospital Insurance
Part B: Medical Expense Insurance
Part C: Medicare Advantage (Medicare + Choice)
Part D: Prescription Drug Program

Financing for the Medicare program comes from three sources: government revenue, premiums from Medicare beneficiaries and

Medicare taxes paid by most working persons and employers.

You can find information on Medicare, Medicare HMOs, Medicare Part D Prescription Drug Program or Medicare supplemental insurance online at www.medicare.gov or by calling toll-free 800-633-4227.

Medicaid

Medicaid provides access to health care for low-income individuals who qualify. Applications for Medicaid and other services are taken at a local office of the Florida Department of Children and Families (DCF). Information on the Medicaid program in Florida can be obtained online at www.dcf.state.fl.us/programs/access/medicaid.shtml.

The Agency for Health Care Administration (AHCA) provides information on Medicaid covered services. Information may be obtained online at www.state.fl.us/cf_web. For a list of locations and phone numbers of AHCA Medicaid area offices, go to ahca.myflorida.com/Medicaid/Areas/index.shtml or call toll-free 888-419-3456.

SHINE Program

Serving Health Insurance Needs of Elders (SHINE) is a free, volunteer-based health insurance counseling program for seniors administered by the Florida Department of Elder Affairs. Information on Medicare HMO coverage in Florida, as well as other programs and services, can be obtained at www.floridashine.org or by calling 1-800-96-ELDER (1-800-963-5337).

Medicare Part D Prescription Drug Benefit

Medicare Part D is a type of insurance to help people with Medicare pay for prescription drugs. As of January 1, 2006, the Medicare Part D Prescription Drug benefit is provided through Medicare-approved private health plans. If you receive health coverage through Medicare and the Florida Medicaid program, your prescription drugs are covered under the Medicare Part D benefit. If you have Medicare coverage but not Medicaid, you can enroll in a Medicare Part D drug plan, but you are not required to do so.

You should compare the various drug plans, including Medicare Part D, before you choose one to see which ones cover the prescription medicines you take, how much coverage they offer, the cost of deductibles, copayments and the monthly premium, and which pharmacies you can use with each plan.

Florida residents enrolled in Medicare Part A (hospital insurance) and/or Part B (medical insurance) are eligible for the prescription drug coverage (Part D). Additionally, individuals eligible for both Medicare and Medicaid benefits (dual-eligible) may also enroll in the Part D program.

Under the Part D program, a participants out-of-pocket costs for covered medications in 2010 will include:

1. An annual $310 deductible,
2. 25% of prescription costs between $310 and $2,830 (a total of $630), and
3. 100% of prescription costs between $2,830 and $6,440 (a total of $3,610).

Once prescription costs reach $6,440 (a total of $4,550 true out-of-pocket costs – not including the premium), consumers will pay $2.50 for generics and preferred drugs and $6.30 for all other drugs, or a 5% co-pay, whichever is greater.

You can find more information and help with enrollment by calling Medicare's toll-free number 800-633-4227 or by going to its Web site www.Medicare.gov.

You can also call the Florida Elder Care Services (SHINE) toll-free number 800-963-5337. It has trained volunteers who can assist you with questions about the Medicare Part D Prescription Drug benefit.

Alternative Prescription Drug Assistance Programs

Florida residents including children, families and senior citizens also have various alternative programs that can assist them in covering the cost of prescription drugs. Plans for senior citizens are available to individuals with limited incomes and who have both Medicare and Medicaid benefits, Medicare Savings Programs, or Social Security Income (SSI) assistance. A complete list of service providers is available at www.floridashine.org/presassis.html. It is advisable that individuals residing part of the year in Florida consider a plan that provides national coverage.

The state of Florida also provides a discount drug card for residents who are:

- Age 60 to 64, without prescription drug coverage, and do not belong to a Medicare Part D plan; or
- Under age 60, without prescription drug coverage and with an annual family income of less than 300% of the federal poverty level. Qualifying incomes include:
  - $32,490 per year for an individual
  - $43,710 per year for a family of two
  - $66,150 per year for a family of four

Download a card at www.floridadiscountdrugcard.net.

Working with the Agency for Healthcare Administration, Florida's Office of Attorney General also provides a dedicated Web site to help consumers shop for the lowest prescription price in their area. You can search by county and drug name at www.myfloridarx.com.

Florida KidCare Program

KidCare is a Florida health insurance program for children that provides medical coverage at low or no cost, depending on family income. Information may be obtained at www.floridakidcare.org or by calling toll-free 888-540-5437.

County Resources

Healthcare and prescription assistance can also be found through many local health departments and non-profit programs. For example, in Collier County, the Physician Led Access Network (PLAN), a Collier County Medical Society-initiated program that coordinates specialty health care for low-income working residents, partnered with the local health department to offer the Physician's Rx Care. This valuable prescription plan provides residents without insurance discounted rates for prescriptions and medical supplies. Discover more at www.plancc.org.

Health Care Resources

To obtain tips on various health care programs available in Florida and to compare the benefits and costs of those programs, go to Family Health Budget at www.familyhealthbudget.com/basics/comparison.asp.

Health Maintenance Organizations

Health Maintenance Organizations (HMOs) are a type of health insurance plan regulated by the Agency for Health Care Administration (AHCA) and the Department of Financial Services. To find out more, go to the AHCA Web site at ahca.myflorida.com/MCHQ/Managed_Health_Care/index.shtml

The Florida HMO Report includes a list of specific HMOs serving different areas of Florida, a summary of the various HMO services and the results of a member satisfaction survey. It is available at www.FloridaHealthFinder.gov, or you can order a copy by calling toll-free 888-419-3456.

Florida Nursing Home Guide

The Nursing Home Guide provides advice for choosing a Florida nursing home, including which insurance payments are accepted by which nursing homes. It also has a rating system using common criteria to assess nursing home quality. Instructions on how to interpret, use and download the guide are available at apps.ahca.myflorida.com/NHCGUIDE/ or order it by calling 888-419-3456.

Direct Care Providers/Concierge Medicine

Due to a rise in premiums and a reduction in covered conditions, many residents in Florida are going outside the insurance arena and choosing to pay health care providers directly—to obtain a higher level of service, such as house calls, physician access 24/7, no waiting room time, etc. This type of service is called concierge medicine.

An example of one Florida health care provider with a higher level of service is Naples Health Care Associates in Collier County (www.napleshealthcare.org).

Health Guides for Families and Individuals

Several guides are available from the Agency for Healthcare Administration as a reference to assist consumers in evaluating their healthcare options in Florida. View and download them at www.FloridaHealthFinder.gov.

Long-Term Care Insurance

Floridians are living longer and healthier lives, thanks to better medical care, better diet and safer living and working environments. However, no one is immune from the effects of aging, which often result in reduced mental or physical ability. You or a loved one could need long-term care (LTC) services in your home or elsewhere as a result of aging, a disabling disease or a serious accident—situations that could happen to anyone.

Having family or friends act as caregivers may not always be a realistic option. The alternative is professional LTC services, which may be provided by a health care professional, such as a nurse, a home health aide or other personal care providers on a part-time or full-time basis. The services can be provided in a setting such as your own home, an assisted living facility, an adult day care center or a nursing home.

The fact is that six out of ten people age sixty-five years or older will need at least one year of long-term care during their lifetime. With an average stay in a nursing home of over 2.5 years, the cost can be staggering.

Many Florida seniors are shocked when they realize that Medicare will not fully cover their health care costs after retirement, particularly long-term care costs. The reality is that Medicare only covers nursing home costs for a very short period. At best, Medicare will pay for all or part of the first one hundred days of care and only if it follows a hospital stay to recuperate from an acute illness or injury. Anyone with even a passing experience with Alzheimer's disease, stroke, Parkinson's disease or simply elder frailty can appreciate the severity and financial devastation of these all too common life events. The following table displays the statistics on the length of care needed for major illnesses frequently requiring long-term care.

Leading Causes for LTC	Length of Care
Alzheimer's disease	96 months
Cancer	36 months
Cardiac Conditions	16 months
Diabetes	48 months
Pulmonary Conditions	36 months
Stroke	21 months

According to the MetLife Mature Market Institute®, the national average rates in 2009 for a private room in a Florida nursing home was $236 daily. At a compounded annual inflation rate of 5 percent, the LTC costs in 2016 would be over $115,000 per year. In fact, failure to plan for LTC is the number-one cause of poverty among older Americans. The best way to be prepared for the cost of LTC is to purchase LTC insurance.

When purchasing LTC insurance, you should consider four basic components in your decision:

- Benefit amount: The maximum fixed-dollar amount that a policy will pay each day.
- Inflation adjustment: The increase in the benefit amount to cover the effect of inflation.
- Benefit period: The length of time an LTC policy will pay for covered services (e.g., two years to unlimited time).
- Elimination period: The number of days that you pay for covered services before the policy pays (e.g., 30-, 60-, 90-, 120- or 365-day period).

To learn more about your choices, contact an LTC agent who is licensed to do business in Florida.

When shopping for an appropriate long-term care insurance policy, financial strength is a key consideration. There are several established insurer rating services, such as A.M. Best Company (ambest.com), Fitch, Inc. (fitchratings.com), Moody's Investor Service, Inc. (moodys.com), Standard & Poor's Insurance Rating Services (standardandpoors.com) and Weiss Research, Inc. (weissinc. com). Visit them online or go to your local Florida public library.

In addition to ratings, the reputation of an insurer is also important. You can contact the Florida Insurance Commissioner regarding an insurance company's status and any complaints from policyholders. In addition you may obtain a copy of "A Shopper's Guide to Long Term Care Insurance" from the National Association of Insurance Commissioners online at https://eapps.naic.org/forms/ipsd/Consumer_info.jsp or by phone at (816) 783-8300.

If you are contemplating purchasing health insurance, you should verify whether the company is authorized to do business in Florida. In most cases, the benefits of authorized Florida insurers are guaranteed through the Florida Insurance Guarantee Association (FIGA) and the Florida Life and Health Insurance Guaranty Association (FLHIGA) which provide the following:

- FIGA pays the claims of property and casualty authorized insurers if the company becomes insolvent and cannot pay.
- FLHIGA pays the claims of life and health authorized insurers if the company becomes insolvent and cannot pay.

If you purchase insurance from a company that is not authorized to do business in Florida, you run the risk of not having the above protections.

When selecting an agent to help you purchase the correct insurance, you should choose one who is licensed to sell insurance in Florida as well as an agent you feel comfortable with who will be available to answer your questions, handle your policy and provide on-going service.

Healthcare Information Resources

Find any type of health care facility in Florida—including hospitals, home health agencies, nursing homes, assisted living facilities, skilled nursing centers and hospices—at floridahealthfinder.cloudapp.net/facilitylocator/facloc.aspx. The Florida Hospital Association also lists hospitals and health systems throughout Florida at www.fha.org/hospdir.html. There are many publications and other resources available to help you with information on health insurance issues, including the American Association of Retired Persons (AARP) which has information on health insurance for seniors at http://www.aarp.org/health/medicare-insurance/.

Additional information on health insurance companies and consumer insurance guides may be obtained from any of the following sources:

- Florida Department of Financial Services, Consumer help line, 1-800-342-2762
- Office of Insurance Regulation, www.floir.com
- Florida Department of Financial Services Consumer Guides, www.myfloridacfo.com/Consumers/needourhelp. htm or 1-877-MY-FL-CFO (1-877-693-5236).

FLORIDA'S ECONOMIC STRENGTHS

International trade: 40 percent of all U.S. exports to Latin and South America pass through Florida.

Tourism: 80.3 million visitors in 2009. The tourism industry has an economic impact of about $50 billion on Florida's economy each year.

Space industry: The space industry contributes $4.5 billion to the state's economy.

Agriculture: Florida is second only to Brazil in global orange juice production. More than 90 percent of America's orange juice is made from Florida-grown oranges.

Construction: This industry's strength results from the steady stream of new residents and visitors who are welcomed to Florida each year.

University research: More than $500 million per year in sponsored research at Florida universities.

Source: Florida Dept. of State; www.myflorida.com; U.S. Census Bureau; and the Bureau of Economic & Business Research (University of Florida).

"It's not your traditional report. I've done it in the form of a YouTube video."

The things taught in schools and colleges are not an education,
but the means to an education.
— Ralph Waldo Emerson

CHAPTER 12

FLORIDA EDUCATION

Educational opportunities abound throughout Florida. Whether you are 3, 33 or 83, there are programs available to further your knowledge, creativity and enjoyment of this great state. From pre-kindergarten to college to adult education, Floridians have endless opportunities to keep busy, keep abreast and to continue learning and growing.

Early Years

In Florida, before a child enters into kindergarten, each school is required to administer a kindergarten readiness screening. In 2005, the Florida Voluntary Prekindergarten (VPK) legislation was signed into law by then-Governor Jeb Bush. This law created a program to prepare every Florida four-year-old for kindergarten and to build a strong foundation for their continued educational success. The program is free (at participating schools) and participation is voluntary. For more information on VPK and early learning/prekindergarten, visit www.vpkhelp.org or www.fldoe. org/earlylearning.com/. It is up to the parents to decide if they want to use the voluntary prekindergarten program or choose a program of their own, such as a Montessori school or another type of private school.

Benefits of early education and the VPK program include:

- The most important growth and development in the brain happens by the age of five.
- The early years are the learning years. A child's ability to be attentive and to follow directions emerges in the early years. Structured early learning fosters these abilities for later success in school and in life.
- Pre-K prepares children to be ready for school. Children who participate in high-quality early childhood education programs develop better language skills, score higher in school-readiness tests and have better social skills and fewer behavioral problems once they enter school. They are also better prepared for kindergarten, especially in the areas of pre-reading, pre-math and social skills.
- Pre-K promotes a love of learning in children, enhances what a child learns at home and instills a love of life-long learning.

GEOGRAPHY: THE FLORIDA PANHANDLE

The boundaries of what is considered the Florida panhandle run from Florida's western border with Alabama east to Lake City. Major cities in the panhandle include Pensacola, Tallahassee, Apalachicola and Fort Walton Beach. Colorful fishing towns line the coast which is also a major attraction for surfers. Tallahassee is the state capital and is home to Florida State University. Hunting, fishing and hiking opportunities abound in vast forests and, for a change of pace, there's Florida Caverns State Park, one of the only dry caves in Florida.

Highlights of the VPK Program

FREE for all children who live in Florida and turn 4 years of age by September 1. There is no registration fee and parents can enroll a child in either a participating child care or public school provider. However, transportation is not provided so it's the parents responsibility to get their child to and from a VPK school. The curriculum focuses on reading, writing and social skills as well as prepares children for kindergarten. VPK programs also provide early language and literacy development.

VPK Program Options

- Option 1: School-year VPK – 540 instructional hours.
- Option 2: Summer VPK – 300 instructional hours.

FACTS ABOUT THE FLORIDA PANHANDLE

DeFuniak Springs is home to one of the two naturally round lakes in the world.

Dr. John Gorrie of Apalachicola invented mechanical refrigeration and air conditioning in 1851.

Some cities and counties are in Eastern Time Zone, but most are in Central Time Zone.

The famous Blue Angels flight demonstration team make their home in Pensacola.

The National Museum of Naval Aviation is located in Warrington.

Some Tarzan movies featuring Johnny Weissmuller and Maureen O'Sullivan were filmed at Wakulla Springs.

VPK Provider Expectations

Parents have the option of choosing a provider that meets their family's needs. These include private and faith-based child care centers, private and public schools and licensed family child care homes. All VPK providers must meet high standards required by law.

Class size does not exceed 18 children in the school-year program and 10 children for the summer program. Plus, all VPK instructors must have a minimum of a child development associate's degree for the school-year program or a bachelor's degree in early childhood or related fields for the summer program.

Primary and Secondary Education

In Florida, K-12 students and parents are afforded the right to education choice. Whether parents live in a school district that offers school choice, are changing residences or have a child entering kindergarten, choosing a school is a complex decision that includes the characteristics of the child, family and schools. These choices include public school, private school, home education and private tutoring. To learn more about the different types of educational choices in Florida go to www.fldoe.org or www.floridaschoolchoice.org.

Public K-12 schools in Florida are individually ranked based on data from the Florida Comprehensive Assessment Test (FCAT) provided by the Florida Department of Education. You can search school rankings at www.greatschools.org/florida/.

The No Child Left Behind (NCLB) law means states and school districts must provide "report cards" for parents. The information is tailored for parents telling them about the quality of education at their child's school. Written in an easy-to-read format, these report cards ensure that parents and taxpayers know which schools are achieving and how. Included in the report cards are student achievement data broken out by race, ethnicity, gender, English language proficiency, as well as breakouts by whether the students are immigrants or have disabilities and whether they are disadvantaged. States and school districts must also provide parents and children in struggling schools timely notification of the public school choice and supplemental services options that may be available for their children.

Post-Secondary Education

There are ten public universities and a liberal arts college that comprise the State University System of Florida. In addition, the Florida College System includes 28 public community colleges and state colleges. Florida also has many private universities, some of which comprise the Independent Colleges and Universities of Florida.

State University System

The state university system is comprised of 11 institutions. Below is a list of the different universities that make up the state system:

- Florida Agricultural and Mechanical University (Tallahassee)
- Florida Atlantic University (Boca Raton)
- Florida Gulf Coast University (Fort Myers)
- Florida International University (Miami)
- Florida State University (Tallahassee)
- New College of Florida (Sarasota)
- University of Central Florida (Orlando)
- University of Florida (Gainesville)
- University of North Florida (Jacksonville)
- University of South Florida (Tampa)
- University of West Florida (Pensacola)

Florida College System

Florida's colleges remain the primary point of access to higher education in Florida, with 66 percent of the state's high school graduates pursuing postsecondary education beginning at a Florida

IN-STATE TUITION POLICY

As stated in Florida Statute § 240.1201: To be classified as a "resident for tuition purposes," a person, or, if a dependent child, the child's parent or parents, shall have established legal residence in Florida and **shall have maintained legal residence in Florida for at least twelve (12) consecutive months immediately prior to his or her initial enrollment.**...Every applicant for admission to a university shall be required to make a statement as to the length of residence in the state and, shall also establish his or her presence, or, if a dependent child, the presence of his or her parent or parents, in the state for the purpose of maintaining a bona fide domicile in accordance with the provisions of the statute.

....

An individual shall **not** be classified as a resident for tuition purposes and, thus, shall **not** be eligible to receive the resident tuition rate, until the individual has provided satisfactory evidence as to his or her legal residence and domicile to appropriate university officials. In determining residency, the university shall require evidence such as:

- A Florida voter's registration card.
- A Florida driver's license.
- A State of Florida identification card.
- A Florida vehicle registration.
- Proof of a permanent home in Florida which is occupied as a primary residence by the individual or by the individual's parent if the individual is a dependent child.
- Proof of a homestead exemption in Florida.
- Transcripts from a Florida high school for multiple years if the Florida high school diploma or GED was earned within the last 12 months.
- Proof of permanent full-time employment in Florida for at least 30 hrs/week for a 12-month period.
- A declaration of domicile in Florida.
- A Florida professional or occupational license.
- Florida incorporation.
- A document evidencing family ties in Florida.
- Proof of membership in a Florida-based charitable or professional organization.
- Any other documentation that supports the student's request for resident status, including, but not limited to, utility bills and proof of 12 consecutive months of payments; a lease agreement and proof of 12 consecutive months of payments; or an official state, federal, or court document evidencing legal ties to Florida.

Source: Florida Statute § 240.1201, Determination of resident status for tuition purposes. Read the entire statute online at http://www.leg.state.fl.us/.

college and 81 percent of freshman and sophomore minority students in public higher education attending one of Florida's 28 colleges. Here they are:

- Brevard Community College (Cocoa)
- Broward College (Davie)
- Chipola College (Marianna)
- College of Central Florida (Ocala)
- Daytona State College (Daytona Beach)
- Edison State College (Fort Myers)
- Florida State College at Jacksonville (Jacksonville)
- Florida Keys Community College (Key West)
- Gulf Coast Community College (Panama City)
- Hillsborough Community College (Tampa)
- Indian River State College (Ft. Pierce)
- Lake City Community College (Lake City)
- Lake-Sumter Community College (Leesburg)
- Miami Dade College (Miami)
- North Florida Community College (Madison)
- Northwest Florida State College (Niceville)
- Palm Beach State College (Lake Worth)
- Pasco-Hernando Community College (New Port Richey)
- Pensacola State College (Pensacola)
- Polk State College (Winter Haven)
- Santa Fe College (Gainesville)
- Seminole State College of Florida (Sanford)
- South Florida Community College (Avon Park)
- St. Johns River Community College (Palatka)
- St. Petersburg College (St. Petersburg, Florida)
- State College of Florida, Manatee-Sarasota (Bradenton)
- Tallahassee Community College (Tallahassee)
- Valencia Community College (Orlando)

Private Colleges and Universities

The Independent Colleges and Universities of Florida (ICUF) is an association of 28 private education institutions in the state of

Florida. Here is a list of them:

- Barry University (Miami Shores)
- Beacon College (Leesburg)
- Bethune-Cookman University (Daytona Beach)
- Clearwater Christian College (Clearwater)
- Eckerd College (St. Petersburg)
- Edward Waters College (Jacksonville)
- Embry-Riddle Aeronautical University (Daytona Beach)
- Flagler College (St. Augustine)
- Florida College (Temple Terrace)
- Florida Hospital College of Health Science (Orlando)
- Florida Institute of Technology (Melbourne)
- Florida Memorial University (Miami)
- Florida Southern College (Lakeland)
- Hodges University (Naples)
- Jacksonville University (Jacksonville)
- Lynn University (Boca Raton)
- Nova Southeastern University (Davie)
- Palm Beach Atlantic University (West Palm Beach)
- Ringling College of Art and Design (Sarasota)
- Rollins College (Winter Park)
- Saint Leo University (St. Leo)
- Saint Thomas University (Miami Gardens)
- Southeastern University (Lakeland)
- Stetson University (Deland)
- University of Miami (Coral Gables)
- University of Tampa (Tampa)
- Warner University (Lake Wales)
- Webber International University (Babson Park)

Additionally, there are 20 colleges and universities that are not affiliated with the ICUF, but are fully-accredited universities in the state of Florida. They are:

- Ave Maria University (Ave Maria)
- Baptist College of Florida (Graceville)

- Carlos Albizu University (Miami)
- Digital Media Arts College (Boca Raton)
- Everest University (Pompano Beach)
- Everglades University (Boca Raton)
- Florida Christian College (Kissimmee)
- Fort Lauderdale Institute of Art (Fort Lauderdale)
- Full Sail University (Winter Park)
- Hobe Sound Bible College (Hobe Sound)
- Johnson & Wales University (North Miami)
- Jones College (Jacksonville)
- Miami International University of Art & Design (Sarasota)
- Northwood University (West Palm Beach)
- Orlando Culinary Academy (Orlando)
- Pensacola Christian College (Pensacola)
- Rasmussen College (Holiday, Ocala, Fort Myers)
- Saint John Vianney College Seminary (Miami)
- Schiller International University (Largo)
- Trinity College (Temple Terrace)

Scholarships and Financial Aid

There are a number of different scholarships and grants available for Florida residents to further their education. One of the most popular among graduating high school seniors is the Florida Bright Futures Scholarship. In 1997, the Florida Legislature created the Florida Bright Futures Scholarship Program to reward students for their academic achievements during high school by providing funding to attend postsecondary education facilities in Florida.

The Florida Bright Futures Scholarship Program is comprised of the following three awards:

- Florida Academic Scholars (FAS) award – including Academic Top Scholars (ATS) award
- Florida Medallion Scholars (FMA) award
- Florida Gold Seal Vocational Scholars (GSV) award

CELEBRITY GRADUATES

Steve "Lefty" Carlton – Born on December 22, 1944, in Miami, Steve was regarded as the best pitcher in baseball history. His left handed pitching and bowling gave him the nickname "Lefty." Steve Carlton completed high school at North Miami. While at Miami-Dade Community College, Steve received recognition while pitching and signed with the St. Louis Cardinals. Carlton also played for the Philadelphia Phillies, Chicago White Sox, San Francisco Giants, Cleveland Indians and the Minnesota Twins. He was inducted into the Baseball Hall of Fame in 1994, 12 years after his retirement.

Edgerrin James – Born October 1, 1978, in Immokalee, Florida, James attended Immokalee High School where he was a football player. He was named as a Parade All-American. James was recruited by the University of Miami where he proved to be one of the most successful running backs in the school's history. After college James was selected in the first round of the 1999 NFL Draft by the Indianapolis Colts. After seven seasons with the Colts, James played for the Arizona Cardinals and the Seattle Seahawks. Edgerrin founded the Edgerrin James Foundation and has donated money to the University of Miami athletics department and also to his former high school.

Jim Morrison – James Douglas, aka Jim Morrison, is regarded as a very important name in the history of rock music. After attending high school in Alexandria, Morrison completed his education at St. Petersburg College and Florida State University. He was the face of The Doors, a music group he formed with his friends in college. Jim's career also includes filmmaking, writing songs, poetry and books.

Ben Vereen – Born on October 10, 1946, in Miami, Ben is a flamboyant actor, dancer and singer. While his education began in Florida, Ben completed it at Manhattan High School of Performing Arts.

CELEBRITY GRADUATES

Harry T. Moore – Born on November, 18, 1905, in Houston, Florida, Harry Moore was the only civil activist who died defending civil rights of blacks. Harry educated himself in Jacksonville and graduated from Florida Memorable College. After graduation, he became a full-time educator.

Norman E. Thagard – Born on July 3, 1949, in Marianna, Florida, Norman Thagard considers his home town as Jacksonville. Dr. Thagard is an astronaut with NASA and was the first American cosmonaut (an astronaut traveling in the Russian vehicle/spacecraft). Norman graduated from Paxon Senior High School in Jacksonville in 1961 and acquired his bachelors and masters of science in engineering from Florida State University; he went on to earn his Doctorate in medicine from the University of Texas. Thagard was awarded 11 Air Medals, the Navy Commendation medal with combat "V," the Marine Corps "E" Award, the Vietnam Service Medal, and the Vietnamese Cross of Gallantry with Palm.

Terry Gene Bollea "Hulk Hogan" – Born August 11, 1953, Hulk Hogan was raised in Tampa and attended the University of South Florida. He is an American professional wrestler, actor, television personality and musician currently signed to Total Nonstop Action Wrestling. Hogan was inducted into the WWE Hall of Fame in 2005. He is a twelve-time world heavyweight champion, a six-time WWF/E Champion and a six-time WCW World Heavyweight champion, as well as a former World Tag Team champion with Edge. He was the first wrestler to win the WWE Championship three times. He was also the winner of the Royal Rumble in 1990 and 1991 and the first to win two Royal Rumbles in a row.

CELEBRITY GRADUATES

James Weldon Johnson – Born on June 17, 1871, in Jacksonville, James was an author and educator. The son of the first black female teacher, James had a keen interest in education. After completing his schooling from Edwin M. Stanton School in Florida, James acquired his associate bachelor's degree from Atlanta University. James served in the education field by working as a Principal of the Jacksonville school for blacks. He was the first African-American to qualify for the Florida bar exam. In his later life, James involved himself as an author, politician, diplomat, critic, journalist, poet, anthologist, lawyer, songwriter and early civil rights activist.

Erin Andrews – Born May 4, 1978, in Lewiston, Maine, Andrews moved to Tampa as a young girl. After attending Bloomingdale High School near Tampa, Andrews graduated in 2000 from the University of Florida with a degree in telecommunications. After graduation, Andrews began work as a freelance reporter for FSN Florida, the Sunshine Network, serving as a Tampa Bay Lightning reporter and as a studio host and part-time reporter for Turner Sports, covering the Atlanta Braves and college football for TBS and the Atlanta Thrashers and Hawks for Turner South. In May 2004, she became a reporter for ESPN's National Hockey Leagues. Since then she has served as sideline reporter for their college football Saturday telecast as well as their Saturday Primetime and Big Ten college basketball coverage. In 2005, her job expanded to include Major League Baseball sideline reporting. Andrews was a contestant on the tenth season of *Dancing with the Stars* where she placed third.

CELEBRITY GRADUATES

Julian "Cannonball" Adderley – Born on September 15, 1928, in Tampa, Julian was one of the best jazz saxophonists in 1950-1960. He completed his education from Florida A&M University in 1948 and studied music at the U.S. Naval Academy. Adderley taught applied instrumental music at Dillard High School in Fort Lauderdale. Cannonball was a living legend in Florida until he moved to New York. He was inducted to the Jazz Hall of Fame after his death on August 8, 1975.

Faye Dunaway – Born January 14, 1941, in Bascom, Florida, Dunaway is an actress. She attended the University of Florida, Florida State University and Boston University, but graduated from the University of Florida in theater. In 1976, Dunaway won an Academy Award for Best Actress for her performance in *Network* after receiving previous nominations for the critically acclaimed films *Bonnie and Clyde* and *Chinatown*. She has starred in a variety of films, including *The Thomas Crown Affair*, *The Towering Inferno*, *Three Days of the Condor* and *Mommie Dearest*. Dunaway has a star on the Hollywood Walk of Fame.

Burt Reynolds – Born in Michigan, the Oscar-nominated star who rose to fame as the leading man in *The Longest Yard* and *Smokey and the Bandit*, Burt Reynolds graduated from Palm Beach High School in West Palm Beach, and entered Florida State University on a football scholarship. After a serious knee injury in 1955, Reynolds recuperated on the coast and attended classes at Palm Beach Junior College (now Palm Beach Community College). There, he met an English professor who got him interested in acting. When Reynolds returned to Florida State, he switched his major from athletics to college drama. He won a Florida State Drama Award and was also drafted by an NFL team, the Baltimore Colts, but never ended up playing professional football. In 1958, Reynolds graduated from Florida State.

You can find more information on the Bright Futures Scholarship and additional scholarship programs at www. floridastudentfinancialaid.org, collegescholarships.org/states/ florida.htm and www.flbog.org/forstudents/planning/.

Top 5 Colleges by Enrollment in Florida

Miami Dade College: Miami Dade College is a public four-year college with eight campuses and 21 outreach centers located throughout Miami-Dade County. It is the largest member institution of the Florida College System. Miami Dade College's main campus is in downtown Miami. Founded in 1959 as Dade County Junior College, it is the largest nonprofit institution of higher learning in the United States with over 161,000 students. It is currently the largest secondary institution in the United States in terms of number of students enrolled. Miami Dade College offers degrees for associates and bachelors, programs in vocational trades as well as certifications. The programs offered by this college include accounting, agriculture, atmospheric science & meteorology, building construction, dietetics, business administration, economics, engineering, forestry, pre-law and pre-veterinary medicine.

University of Central Florida: University of Central Florida is a metropolitan public research university located in Orlando. UCF is a member institution of the State University System of Florida and is currently the largest university in the state and the third largest university in the United States by enrollment. UCF is a space-grant university and has made noted research contributions to optics, modeling and simulation, digital media, engineering and computer science, business administration, education, and hospitality management. It is considered to be the 70th best up-and-coming national university by *U.S. News and World Report*. University of Central Florida offers bachelors, masters and doctoral degrees in various fields. The programs include diversity, business, accounting, social sciences and education. Founded in 1963 as Florida Technological University, this school's original goal was to provide highly-trained personnel to support the Kennedy Space Center. As the university's academic scope expanded to encompass other disciplines, the school was renamed the University of Central Florida in 1978.

University of Florida: University of Florida is an American public land-grant, sea-grant, space-grant research university located on a 2,000-acre campus in Gainesville. The university traces its origins to 1853 and has operated continuously on its present Gainesville campus since September 1906. UF is currently ranked 53rd overall in national universities, public and private, and ranks among the world's top 100 universities. It is the second largest Florida university by student population and the most academically prestigious university in the state of Florida, as measured by national and international rankings of American colleges and universities. It is also one of the most academically diverse in the nation, as measured by the number of academic programs offered and is home to 17 academic colleges and more than 150 research centers and institutes. The school offers multiple graduate professional programs including business administration, engineering, law and medicine on one contiguous campus, and administers 123 master's degree programs and 76 doctoral degree programs in 87 schools and departments.

University of South Florida: The University of South Florida is a member institution of the State University System of Florida and is one of the state's three flagship universities. It is a public research university located in Tampa with an autonomous campus in St. Petersburg and branch centers in Sarasota and Lakeland. Founded in 1956, USF is the ninth largest university in the nation and the third largest in the state of Florida. The programs offered at University of South Florida include business, education, criminal justice, engineering, music, nursing, law, medicine, social work, human services and communication. USF has 18 colleges, schools and institutions.

Florida State University: Florida State University is a space-grant and sea-grant public university located in Tallahassee. It is a comprehensive doctoral research university with medical programs. The university comprises 15 separate colleges and 39 centers, facilities, labs and institutes that offer more than 300 programs of study, including professional programs. Florida State is a flagship university in the State University System of Florida. As one of Florida's primary graduate research universities, Florida State awards over 2,000 graduate and professional degrees each year. Florida State University is home to nationally ranked programs in many academic areas, including the sciences, social policy, film, engineering, the arts, business, political science, social work, medicine and law. Florida State is home to Florida's only National Laboratory, The National High Magnetic Field Laboratory, and is the birthplace of the commercially-viable, anti-cancer drug Taxol. FSU was officially established in 1851 and is located on the oldest continuous site of higher education in the state of Florida.

TOP 10 FLORIDA EMPLOYERS

The top ten employers in Florida are:

- Hulett Environmental Services (Orlando)
- University of Florida (Gainesville)
- Pensacola Naval Air Station (Pensacola)
- Florida Hospital (Orlando)
- Orlando Regional Healthcare (Orlando)
- City of Jacksonville (Jacksonville)
- Broward County Commissioners (Fort Lauderdale)
- Lee Memorial Health System (Fort Myers)
- Shands Hospital (Gainesville)
- Florida Hospital Center (Orlando)

Florida Careers

The Sunshine State can boast, not only of its warm weather and beautiful beaches, but also of a job growth rate that is more than double the national average and a very low unemployment rate. Nearly every major industry is experiencing growth in Florida. The areas with the largest number of new jobs in Florida are Miami/Fort Lauderdale, Orlando and Tampa/St. Petersburg.

Jobs in Technology and Computers

Technology careers are booming in Florida. The top seven jobs expected to experience significant growth by 2011 are computer software specialists, computer software applications engineers, network administrators, computer systems software engineers, desktop publishers, systems analysts and database administrators.

Jobs in Health Care

Health and medical professionals are in high demand in Florida. According to *The Orlando Sentinel* (www.orlandosentinel.com), the positions in greatest demand are physician assistants, medical assistants, medical records and health information technicians, physical therapy aides, respiratory therapy technicians, occupational therapy assistants, home health aides, registered nurses, pharmacy technicians, and mental health and substance abuse social workers.

Jobs in Construction Trades

The construction field is the second fastest growing in the State of Florida with project managers in particularly high demand. Other hot job prospects are available for electricians, carpenters, mechanics, plasterers, concrete finishers, drywall installers, lathers and laborers.

APPENDIX A
ONLINE RESOURCES

STATE INFORMATION

The Official Web Site for the State of Florida: www.myflorida.com

Current Facts on Florida: www.flheritage.com/facts

Florida Official Vacation Guide Web Site: www.visitflorida.com

Florida Chamber of Commerce: www.floridachamber.com

Florida Realtors: www.floridarealtors.org

Florida Weather & Hurricane Center: www.nhc.noaa.gov

Florida Division of Emergency Management: www.floridadisaster.org

Change of Mailing Address: https://moversguide.usps.com

Division of Elections: http://election.dos.state.fl.us/

State Parks: http://www.floridastateparks.org/

LOCAL INFORMATION

Florida Churches: www.churchangel.com/florida.htm

Florida Cities: www.floridaleagueofcities.com

Florida Counties: www.myfloridacounty.com/countyportals/

Clerk of Courts Listing:
www.myfloridacounty.com/services/officialrecords_intro.shtml

Boating

Florida Boating Safety: www.FloridaBoatingCourse.com

Safety Equipment Requirements for Florida Watercraft:
www.myfwc.com

Business

Doing Business in Florida: www.eflorida.com/default.asp

Florida Business Guide: www.floridabusinessguide.com

Employment and Labor Issues: www.floridajobs.org

Career Opportunities:

www.stateofflorida.com

www.jobs.careerbuilder.com

www.findjob.net

www.floridacareers.com

www.floridajobs.org

http://florida.preferredjobs.com

https://jobs.myflorida.com

Education

Florida Department of Education: www.fldoe.org

Florida Residency for Tuition Purposes:

www.facts.org/html/residencyGuidelines.html

http://www.leg.state.fl.us/

Florida Department of Education, Student Financial Assistance:
www.floridastudentfinancialaid.org

Florida Scholarships: www.floridastudentfinancialaid.org

K-12 (by County): http://www.fldoe.org/Schools/schoolmap/
flash/schoolmap_text.asp

Community Colleges: http://data.fldoe.org/workforce/contacts/
default.cfm?action=showList&ListID=52

Public School Rankings: www.greatschools.org/florida/

Public Universities: http://www.flbog.org/aboutus/universities/

Volunteer Pre-Kindergarten: www.vpkhelp.org or
www.fldoe.org/earlylearning.com/

Emergency Management

Shelters/Evacuation Routes:

http://www.floridadisaster.org/DEMpublic.asp

Post-Disaster Assistance: www.disasterassistance.gov

Report a Wildfire: (850) 413-9900

Fishing/Hunting

Fishing License Information:
> http://myfwc.com/License/LicPermit_RecreationalHF.htm

Fish & Wildlife Conservation Commission: www.myfwc.com

Freshwater Fishing:
> http://myfwc.com/RECREATION/FW_index.htm

Saltwater Fishing:
> http://myfwc.com/RECREATION/Saltwater_index.htm.

Hunting in Florida:
> http://myfwc.com/recreation/hunt_index.aspx

Health

Health Insurance, Office of Insurance Regulation:
> www.floir.com

Insurance Companies: www.floir.com/companysearch/

Health Care Facilities: www.FloridaHealthFinder.gov

Health Care Information: www.fdhc.state.fl.us

Hospitals and Health Systems: www.fha.org/hospdir.html

Health Care Assistance for Children:
> Florida Kid Care: www.floridakidcare.org
> Healthy Kids: www.healthykids.org

Senior Pharmacy Resources/Prescription Drug Assistance:
> www. FloridaHealthFinder.gov

Motor Vehicles

Driver License Offices: www.hsmv.state.fl.us/offices

First-Time Drivers: www.firsttimedriver.com

Department of Highway Safety &Motor Vehicles:
> www.hsmv.state.fl.us

SunPass: www.sunpass.com

Vehicle Tags and Registration:
> www.hsmv.state.fl.us/html/titlinf.html

Traffic School: www.floridadrivingcourse.com

Plants/Animals

Plants, Florida Department of Agriculture and Consumer
Services: www.doacs.state.fl.us/onestop/

Pets and Other Animals: www.doacs.state.fl.us

Taxes, Finances, Property Insurance
> Florida Department of Revenue: www.myflorida.com/dor
> Florida Taxes/Florida Tax Guide:
>> www.myflorida.com/dor/gta.html
> Department of Revenue, Business Division:
>> www.myflorida.com/dor/businesses
> Florida Tax-Related Information or Questions:
>> www.myflorida.com/dor
> Department of Financial Services, Consumer Guides:
>> www.fldfs.com
> Florida Statutes: www.flsenate.gov/statutes
> Citizens Property Insurance Corporation:
>> www.citizensfla.com

Voter Registration
> Florida Voter Registration Information:
>> http://election.dos.state.fl.us/voter-registration/voter-reg.
>> shtml

U.S. Government
> Social Security/Medicare: www.ssa.gov/top10.html
> U.S. Citizenship & Immigration Issues: www.uscis.gov
> U.S. Government Forms (FEMA, VA benefits, etc.):
>> www.forms.gov
> Passport (new or renewal): www.travel.state.gov
> Federal Voting Assistance Program: www.fvap.gov

APPENDIX B1
DECLARATION OF FLORIDA DOMICILE - *SAMPLE*

DECLARATION OF DOMICILE

This is my Declaration of Domicile in the State of Florida that I am filing this day in accordance and in conformity with Section 222.17, Florida Statutes.

I hereby declare that I became a bona fide resident of the State of Florida on:

_____(date of arrival)

I am, at the time of making this declaration, a bona fide resident of the State of Florida residing at:

_____   _____   _____
(street and number)   (city)   (zip code)

which place of abode I recognize and intend to maintain as my permanent home, and if I maintain another place or places of abode in some other state or states, I hereby declare that my above-described residence and abode in the State of Florida constitutes my predominant and principal home, and I intend to continue it permanently as such.

I formerly resided at:

_____   _____   _____   _____
(street and number)   (city)   (county)   (state)

and the place or places where I maintain another or other places of abode are as follows:

_____   _____   _____   _____
(street and number)   (city)   (county)   (state)

_____   _____   _____   _____
(street and number)   (city)   (county)   (state)

I understand that, as a legal resident of Florida: I am subject to intangible taxes; I must purchase Florida license plates for motor vehicles, if any, owned by me and /or my spouse; if I drive, I must have a Florida drivers license; if I vote, I must vote in the precint of my legal domicile, and that my estate will be probated in Florida courts.

_____   _____
(Signature)   (Signature)

Print Name_____   Print Name_____

ID Produced_____   ID Produced_____

( ) United States Citizen   ( ) United States Citizen

( ) Citizen of_____   ( ) Citizen of_____

　　Green Card #_____   　　Green Card #_____
　　Date of Issuance_____   　　Date of Issuance_____

STATE OF FLORIDA
COUNTY OF _____
Sworn to and subscribed before me *UNDER OATH* this _____ day of _____, 20____.

_____
Signature of Notary Public, State of Florida

Penalty for perjury: up to five (5) years in state prison and $5000.00 fine: Chapter 837.012, F.S.

APPENDIX B2
FLORIDA HOMESTEAD (AD VALOREM)
TAX EXEMPTION (FORM DR 501) - *SAMPLE*

Florida Department of Revenue

Original Application for Ad Valorem Tax Exemption

DR 501
R. 12/99

Tax Year_____

New ☐   Change ☐   Additional ☐

Property identification number: _____

Applicant/Co-applicant Name and Address:

_____

_____

_____

Legal Description:

_____

_____

_____

Applicant Social Security No.: _____

Co-Applicant Social Security No: _____

NOTE: Disclosure of your social security number is mandatory. It is required by section 196.011 (1), Florida Statutes. The social security number will be used to verify taxpayer identity information, homestead exemption information submitted to property appraisers, and intangible tax information submitted to the Department of Revenue

Permanent Florida residency required as of January 1

$25,000 Homestead exemption*(see additional information)	☐
$500 Widow's exemption	☐
$500 Widower's exemption	☐
$500 Disability exemption	☐
$500 Blind persons exemption	☐
Total and permanent disability exemption-Quadriplegics (Documentation required)	☐
Service connected total and permanent disability exemption (Documentation required)	☐
Exemption for disabled veterans confined to wheelchairs (Documentation required)	☐
Total and permanent disability exemption (Documentation required)	☐

*If you wish to apply for an additional homestead exemption enacted by local ordinance for persons age 65 and older you must file form DR-501SC. However, you must either receive, or apply for, the regular homestead to get the 65 and older additional homestead exemption. If you have already received regular homestead exemption, you do not need to file another form DR-501.

Marital status: ☐ Single   ☐ Married   ☐ Widow   ☐ Divorced   ☐ Widower

Did you file tax exemptions last year? ☐ Yes   ☐ No

Where: _____

If no, your last year's address

Ownership information

Percent of ownership_____   Type of deed _____

Recorded: Book _____   Page _____

Date recorded_____   Date of deed _____

Proof of residences for all owners	Owners	Spouse	Other owner
Give address of each owner not residing on property			
Date you last became a permanent Resident of Florida			
Date of occupancy			
Florida driver license number	(Date)	(Date)	(Date)
Florida vehicle tag number			
Florida voter registration number (if U.S. citizen)	(Date)	(Date)	(Date)
Immigration number (Alien Card-if not a U.S. citizen)	(Date)	(Date)	(Date)
Declaration of domicile	Res. date	Res. date	Res. date
Date of birth			
Current employer			
Address listed on your last IRS return			

I hereby authorize this agency to obtain information necessary to determine my eligibility for the exemption(s) applied for. NOTE: If all information is not received by March 1", your application will be processed for whatever exemption you qualify for at that date.

I hereby make application for the exemptions indicated and affirm that I do qualify for same under Florida Statutes. I am a permanent resident of the State of Florida and I own and occupy the property described above. I understand that section 196.131(2) Florida Statutes, provides that any person who knowingly and willfully gives false information for the purpose of claiming homestead exemption is guilty of a misdemeanor of the first degree, punishable by a term of imprisonment not exceeding 1 year or a fine not exceeding $5,000 or both. Further, under penalties of perjury, I declare that I have read the foregoing application and the facts in it are true.

_____   _____

Signature of co-applicant   Signature of co-applicant

_____   _____

Date   Phone number

For Official Use Only

_____

Signature of deputy

_____

Entered by

INDEX

NOTES

Meet Mike Kilbourn

With over 30 years experience in the financial services industry, the last 19 of which have been dedicated to teaching his estate planning strategies to high-net worth families and fellow planners, E. Michael Kilbourn knows the intricacies of estate planning and the benefits of Florida domicile.

The president of Kilbourn Associates in Naples, Florida, Mike is a Family Wealth Transfer Planning Specialist who enjoys taking the worry out of wealth and the mystery out of financial planning.

Over the years, Mike has positioned himself as a leading national authority on estate tax matters and expert on the complexities of Florida domicile. His sophisticated estate planning abilities have produced remarkable results and secured the trust of hundreds of wealthy individuals and families.

Mike is a decorated Vietnam veteran with five college degrees including four masters' degrees, cum laude, and was inducted into Beta Gamma Sigma. Accredited with fourteen professional designations including Chartered Financial Consultant and Accredited Estate Planner, he is founder and chairman of the Wealth Protection Network®, a national network of estate planning professionals.

In addition to authoring the first and second editions of *The Florida Domicile Handbook*, Mike is also the author of *Disinherit the IRS* (Career Press 2003) and contributing author of *Optimal Aging Manual* (Optimal Aging, LLC, 2004), *Giving–Philanthropy for Everyone* (Quantum Press, 2002), *21st Century Wealth: Essential Financial Planning Principles* (Quantum Press, 2000) and *Ways & Means: Maximize the Value of Your Retirement Savings* (Esperti Peterson Institute, 1999).

E. Michael Kilbourn, CLU, ChFC, CCIM, MSFS, CAP, CASL, MBA
Kilbourn Associates
3033 Riviera Drive, Suite 202
Naples, FL 34103
Ph: (239) 261-1888
Fax: (239) 643-7017
Email: mike@kilbournassociates.com
Website: www.kilbournassociates.com

Meet Brad Galbraith

Brad A. Galbraith is a partner with Hahn, Loeser & Parks LLP in Naples, Florida, and co-partner-in-charge of the firm's Indianapolis office. His practice focuses exclusively on providing creative, cutting-edge estate, tax and business planning advice to business owners and other wealthy individuals. Brad is board certified in Wills, Trusts and Estates by the Florida Bar Association.

Brad began his professional career as a Certified Public Accountant. After switching to the practice of law and seeing the ineffectiveness and inefficiency of traditional planning methods, he endeavored to find a better way to assist his clients with estate, tax and business planning. As an estate planning attorney, he developed a model designed to provide clients with comprehensive, personalized estate, tax and business succession plans that withstand the test of time.

Brad maintains an Indiana CPA license and is a frequent presenter on estate and tax planning topics to CPAs and attorneys at conferences and continuing education events throughout the United States. Additionally, Brad is the coauthor of an extensive continuing education program for CPAs, which was published and distributed nationally. That program, titled Estate Planning for CPAs, has been presented to thousands of CPAs throughout the United States.

Brad has been listed in *FIVE STAR: Best in Client Satisfaction Wealth Managers* in 2010. He is active in several national and local charitable and religious organizations as well as organizations that support the arts.

Brad A. Galbraith, Esq, CPA
Board Certified in Wills, Trusts and Estates
Hahn Loeser & Parks LLP
800 Laurel Oak Drive, #600
M&I Building
Naples, Florida 34108
Ph: (239) 552-2990
Fax: (239) 254-2949
Email: bgalbraith@hahnlaw.com
Website: www.hahnlaw.com

Give the Gift of a Better Life in Florida!

Available at your favorite bookstore or purchase additional copies here.

The Florida Domicile Handbook - 2nd Edition is the perfect gift for new homebuyers and new Florida residents!

☐ YES, I want _____ copies of *The Florida Domicile Handbook - 2nd Edition* for $19.95 plus $7.00 for shipping/handling per book.

To Pay By Check

1. Complete the following:

   Name: _____

   Street Address: _____

   City:_____ State (Province): _____

   Zip (Postal) Code:_____ Country: _____

2. Write a check payable to **Brendan Kelly Publishing Inc.** for $19.95 plus $7.00 for shipping/handling for each book purchased.

3. Send a check and this form to: *Brendan Kelly Publishing Inc.*
   2122 Highview Drive
   Burlington, Ontario, Canada L7R 3X4

To Pay By Credit Card

1. Visit our Web site at www.brendankellypublishing.com.

2. Click on ORDER INFO, choose the $US or $CAD order form.

3. Add copy (or copies) of *The Florida Domicile Handbook: Vital Information for New Florida Residents - 2nd Edition* to the shopping cart.

4. Press SECURE CHECKOUT and complete the form.

Discounts on orders larger than 10 books. Call (905) 335-3359 for details.

www.floridadomicilehandbook.com